The Inspirational Story of Ethan A. Poetic

The Inspirational Story of Ethan A. Poetic

The Inspirational Story of Ethan A. Poetic

Chronicles of Adversities, Education, Sports, Relationships, & Resiliency

By

Ethan A. Poetic

The Inspirational Story of Ethan A. Poetic

Chronicles of Adversities, Education, Sports, Relationships, & Resiliency

Ethan A. Poetic

Library of Congress Control Number: TXu-2-334-864

ISBN: Hardcover 979-8-9868472-2-1
Softcover 979-8-9868472-2-1
eBook 979-8-9868472-4-5

Edited by Dante S. McLeod, Ethan A. Poetic, & Trinity Sumrall

Cover Design and Layout by Mekdes G. Woldu

Contact Information

Ethan A. Poetic

Website ethanspeaks.com

creativity, encourages diverse voices, promotes free speech, and narrative.

To order additional copies of this book, contact

Amazon & Ingram sparks

www.amazon.com

www.ingramsparks.com

Barnesandnoble.com

Kobo.com

The Inspirational Story of Ethan A. Poetic

Contents

The Inspirational Story of Ethan A. Poetic

Forewords

Let me start off by saying I am so proud of my cousin Ethan. I remember growing up we both shared a great interest in outdoor activities and sports. If no one knows, Ethan has a vast sports knowledge and like me has always loved the sport of football. As we got a little older, it really sucked being so distant from each other so we couldn't hang out like we typically would. I decided to take off for a career in the military, while Ethan decided to go to college and pursue his dreams. I can clearly think back to the day when I was notified that my cousin had been in a bad accident and I just didn't want to believe it.

In my mind I knew that this couldn't be the end and that he would pull through because I couldn't see it any other way. I'm happy to say that not only did he pull through but I believe it has been a real game changer in his mindset on life and his goals. Ethan continued to pursue his college goals, while simultaneously speaking to the youth about his story which touched people all over. To say I am proud would be an understatement, and I believe when you read this book you will be able to understand why and truly appreciate how amazing of a human being that my cousin Ethan really is.

v/r

IVAN C BOOKARD III

W01, SC

NETWORK SYSTEMS TECHNICIAN

Hub Platoon, SISCO, HHBN, 25ID

The Inspirational Story of Ethan A. Poetic

As the daughter of immigrants and a Hondurican (Honduran and Puerto Rican) in the diaspora, I have always been interested in how far my family extends across the globe, the circumstances that led them there, and how their lives have had an impact on their local communities. Never did I imagine that an Ancestry DNA test would satisfy part of that curiosity and connect me to one of my cousins on the Puerto Rican side — Ethan A. Poetic.

Thanks to technology, we have been able to communicate, exchange, and share in the multifaceted development of our identities and how we see ourselves in the larger narrative of the past, present, and future. When I learned intimately about Ethan's lived experiences (especially across social media), I immediately thought about how other people could read this story in written form and understand what it truly means to survive and thrive to improve not only one's own life outcome but also that of others. Ethan's written life story is what many qualitative researchers would refer to as auto-ethnography.

The Inspirational Story of Ethan A. Poetic

Ethan critically examines his personal experiences in his storytelling and connects his story to the broader meaning of what it means to interrogate the intersection between the self and society. We can use Ethan's story to embrace our own life stories and turn them into a conversation of hope, purpose, and understanding so we can live more fulfilled lives.

Catherine García, PhD

The Inspirational Story of Ethan A. Poetic

I first met Ethan Poetic when he was enrolled as a Millersville University student in my class. I did not know anything about Ethan, other than the fact that he enrolled as a student in our Speech Communication program, and he sat in the same seat every week, on the left side of where I stood. On that first-class meeting, Ethan introduced himself and shook my hand, and said he would stop by my office during office hours if he had any questions. And he did . . . stop by during my office hours each week and ask questions. Sometimes they would be about class assignments and other times he would look around my office at the photos and memorabilia I had collected and ask me questions about those. I knew nothing about his life, and he rarely shared details. I only knew that he used the Ethan A. Poetic pseudonym, when I saw some video interviews he completed during his internship. I thought it was his stage name, a moniker he used for creative work. I have come to learn that the name means much more. Ethan A.

The Inspirational Story of Ethan A. Poetic

Poetic is a name that culminates his life story, and his role as son, stepson, grandson, sibling, step sibling, student, student-athlete, friend, mentor, and inspiration to many. Ethan is a storyteller. I think this was a God-given talent, but I also hope that his time with us at Millersville University helped to hone his storytelling skills a bit more. Ethan Poetic is also honest. I'd go so far as to say, as honest as they come. At one point in the book, Ethan shares, "I knew and believed there was more to life than what I had imagined and was living." This memoir is Ethan's opportunity to tell his story, to recollect and reflect on the historical account of his life, from his perspective and from his personal knowledge. It is also a lesson on a learned subject. The subject is a life constantly in transition. Family transition. Life transition. Medical transition. Health transition. Intellectual transition. Relationship transition. Family was such a big stressor for Ethan, but also a stronghold, in that this was where his greatness started. He was someone who did not feel appreciated or welcomed by much of his family. There was a foundation there, but as Ethan explains, it was "fragile and broken." He firmly believes that God put special people in his life to fill the gaps. Ethan A. Poetic is the man who grew out of that chaotic foundation, with love and acceptance from others. He has found his safe haven and peace, within himself. As he shares, "my testimony is filled with grace, mercy, favor, and a full recovery." And then he adds, "God has a way of doing the unthinkable for those he truly gave a purpose for their life on earth." Much of Ethan's life, has not been poetic. But he was able to see and configure and articulate his life through the art form of poetry. Ethan is the living example of a flower blooming up through cracks in the sidewalk. The roots and growth persevered through the dense bit of dirt, the hard places of sidewalk cement, to grow and bloom. In that same way, Ethan Poetic has bloomed into the Walking, Living Miracle he is today. I hope you find Ethan's story compelling. It is an important read for everyone. He has broken the cycle that he so desperately wanted to break. I'd like to say that you'll enjoy it. But it is difficult to read in places. What you will find, is an authentic story of perseverance and grit and determination. As Ethan shares in his memoir, life is a journey. I, for one, feel blessed, dear Ethan, that our paths crossed during your journey.

Thank you for sharing your story with the world.

Stacey O. Irwin, Ph.D., Ethan's professor
Millersville University of Pennsylvania
Department of Communication & Theatre
Media Arts Production

The Inspirational Story of Ethan A. Poetic

Ethan Poetic has lived a life of triumph through tragedy, steadfastly choosing hope over hopelessness, and finding resilience in both his own inner strength and the boundless power of human connection. His story is a beautiful reminder that courage is forged not by avoiding adversity, but by choosing to rise with grace and dignity every time you're knocked down. A truly remarkable story told with great honesty by a young man who has my deepest respect and admiration.

Jen Janetsky,

Assistant Prosecuting Attorney at Genesee County
Prosecutor's Office

The Inspirational Story of Ethan A. Poetic

As chair of an academic department at a mid-sized state university, I've benefitted from the inspiring stories of students who've graced my classroom and my office and walked through the ordinary ritual of signing up for courses, fulfilling the obligations for those courses, receiving passing grades and moving on to the next academic semester filled with more courses, assignments, exams – until suddenly, the process ends with graduation.

Or – it doesn't.

Indeed, we often assume that college students will complete their coursework as prescribed – and fail to recognize the multiple challenges this simple, "ordinary" process places before our students and the effort it requires of students to complete a degree. Students must plan; they must assemble required financial resources – either from their own reserves, a job, family contributions, or a scholarship – to pay for tuition, books, and supplies. This is all BEFORE the work required during the semester, when planning, financial resources, and the work of reading, completing assignments, studying, applying their knowledge, and building and maintaining relationships in and out of the classroom continues. This "ordinary" process is not for the faint of heart – and statistically, many who begin do not finish.

Throw in additional challenges – a childhood spent living in poverty with and without a father figure, enmeshed in the chaos that results from addiction and domestic violence, responsible for the care for younger siblings, and without the recognition of family for personal accomplishments – and it is remarkable anyone would persist in pursuing the rigors of scholarship through the attainment of a bachelor's degree – and do it with grace, humility, and a mission to share insights with others to encourage them to pursue their own life's purpose.

Yet, Ethan Poetic did attain a Bachelor of Science degree in Speech Communication with a concentration in Media and

Broadcasting in December 2020. He accomplished this with fortitude and patience, even amid a semester during COVID-19, after life lessons from challenges listed above and many others – including homelessness and an event that led him to be named "a walking, living miracle." The many stories Ethan shares in this memoir are coupled with his insights and "teaching moments" as he draws connections between his challenges, the people who stepped up to provide support and mentorship, finding God and inner peace, and re-learning to walk, talk, eat, and do small physical tasks.

His story does not end with graduation and overcoming adversity – but begins, as commencement speakers (and Ethan) remind us. In fact, Ethan reminds us that each day we have the opportunity to live our best life, and he has since launched his own LLC, and continues to write poetry, to author inspirational pieces, to serve as a life coach and to offer motivational speeches and perform spoken word.

In the memoir, he offers the positive teachable moments not only from his own life experience, but from the encounters he's had along the way, whether with coaches, teachers, co-workers, neighbors even someone he happened to meet in the stands at a graduation ceremony. He even shares insights from Lancaster community leaders he interviewed as part of an internship he participated in at Millersville University, offering wisdom from those who themselves not only overcame adversity, but positively impacted their community.

One of the perks of serving in a University is to witness the achievements of individuals who demonstrate the commitment necessary to not only succeed in the classroom, but to redefine "success," and to provide a model for "living your best life" amid constant challenges. I promise that you, too, will be inspired by Ethan's story, and marvel at his positive attitude. I hope that you will find, as I have, that his positive spirit, his attitude of gratitude and humility, will offer you food for thought, gratitude, humility, and appreciation for "ordinary" as well as "extraordinary" accomplishments.

Dr. Theresa Russell-Loretz, Ph.D
Chair and Associate Professor
Department of Communication and Theatre
Millersville University

The Inspirational Story of Ethan A. Poetic

The word that comes to mind when I think about Ethan Poetic and his life story is pertinacious. Ethan has an unwavering persistence about his actions in life. Through struggles and setbacks, he has persevered to build a life and legacy that will live on in all the lives of people he has met. As one life he has touched and someone who has been able to learn his story through a personal friendship, I urge everyone to read his story. When I met Ethan, I was seventeen-year-old high school student just realizing my interests for my future. He supported me through my athletics, and college endeavors. He continues to support me through whatever my next steps in life are. As many say, Ethan is a 'living miracle'. I won't get too in depth on his story, because that is what follows this statement. He is a man that went through a traumatic event in his life. While many would not have survived what he did, he still had a fight ahead of him. Many do not realize that how you treat people can affect their lives. Although many may not have believed Ethan could rebuild his life to what it is today, he knew and believed in himself. He fought to recover. He fought to make his life a success story. God gave Ethan a purpose for his life, and through every obstacle he has adhered to working towards that purpose. Ethan Poetic is here to inspire others who may face adversities in life.

The most inspiring aspect of his story is how he can give back to his community and continue to work to help others through adversities while still advancing in his own life and goals. He is selfless, and that is a rare characteristic in this world. I am still inspired and driven to do better in life by Ethan. I compel all to read his story. To learn from it. And to see how you can make a difference in this world and in others' lives like Ethan has been able to do.

Alyssa Schriver

The Pennsylvania State: Eberly College of Science Alumna

Bachelor's Degree in Biology with a focus in Vertebrate Physiology

The Inspirational Story of Ethan A. Poetic

In the summer of 2001, I met Ethan on the football field at Lancaster McCaskey High School. I was the defensive coordinator at Lancaster McCaskey for 5 years before moving on to become the Head Football Coach at York High School. I lost touch with Ethan during my 5-year stint at York. I became the Head Football Coach at Coatesville in 2009 and learned about Ethan's accident in 2011. I had the incredible opportunity to reconnect with Ethan a couple of years later and our relationship has grown stronger each year. Ethan's story has had an impact on my family, the Coatesville Football and Track Teams and our Coatesville Community. Ethan's willingness to share his journey, his persistent personality and dedication to helping others is what makes his story so valuable. Even when the odds were stacked against him, Ethan persevered, the work ethic that he demonstrated in school and in sports carried over and helped in his rehabilitation process. Once he set his mind to getting better, he did not stop until he did.

The Inspirational Story of Ethan A. Poetic

Ethan's story of miraculous growth and recovery is not to be taken lightly. His story impacts people of all ages and in all stages of life. His story also includes his dedication to his community and the communities around him. He is here to share, to help and to lead others to a life without limits.

Matt Ortega
Head Football Coach
Coatesville Area Senior High School

The Inspirational Story of Ethan A. Poetic

Ethan Poetic's, **The Inspirational Story of Ethan A. Poetic**, is an amazing autobiography that chronicles this young man's journey from tragedy to triumph. Beginning with his early childhood experiences, Ethan boldly shares with us his complicated relationships with family members, including a mother who had multiple relationships and a father who was in and out of his life. From the beginning of the book, he paints a courageously honest picture of his traumas and shows a sophisticated understanding of trauma and its impact: "*There comes a significant cost for allowing children to see an addict self-medicate and submerge in deep underlying pain, wounds, and scars. The world sees very few children brave enough to go against the grain, while the others give into what they experience at home. As children grow up around the world they will often feel the effects of the harmful damage and have severe consequences in their own lives*". Ethan reminds us that the grip of trauma is tight, but with faith, resilience, healthy relationships, and hope, we can loosen the grip and journey towards a life that brings us peace and fulfillment.

Christina G. Watlington, Ph.D.

The Author's Preface

My journey of overcoming the obstacles in my life has been well documented. The symbol of my hardships take place in my childhood. The chronicles of my memoir involve adversities, education, sports, relationships, and resiliency. The structure of a single-parent household has its own dynamics and challenges. In a traditional sense, the normal household consists of two parents. Somewhere along the way in history that structure was broken, leaving future generations to pick up the tab of previous generations without even ordering off the menu. Now true character is revealed during times of adversity. My character was challenged throughout my early upbringing and teenage years, then revealed during adulthood.

Intro

Greetings. You can call me Ethan A. Poetic. I come from an African American, Puerto Rican, and European descent. I am a native of Coatesville, Pennsylvania—home of the Red Raiders of Coatesville Area Senior High School. But I currently reside in Lancaster, Pennsylvania—the Red Rose City, home of the J.P. McCaskey High School Red Tornadoes.

My comeback story is filled with many setbacks that require being a superhero to conquer. While growing up in a low-income, single parent household with minimal resources, I was blessed with great athletic ability, as well as the ability to evolve within my surroundings, and balancing the multiple talents of which I was gifted. I believe that despite my circumstances, I was able to knock down many barriers, which led me to understand that barriers are a universal experience that can evolve into stories of lessons learned.

My story relates to the past, present, and future generations in society. The privileged, underprivileged, and those living in poverty might see parts of themselves in what I've experienced. Furthermore, people going through serious mental health issues with addictions, abuse, and needing a breakthrough in their lives can carry forward some of the lessons I've learned.

But let me warn you, my life as a child, teenager, and adult was not normal.

This memoir explores the negative forces I had to overcome. I will go into detail, in chronological order about my life and the events that have shaped me into the man that I am today. But I must forewarn you that the adversities and hardships I have overcome may shock some readers.

The term "walking, living miracle" can be an inspiring, breathtakingly extraordinary concept to understand. As a matter of fact, the definition states that this refers to someone who has experienced a supernatural miracle and has lived to tell about it as living proof. I have given much deep thought to this concept for over a decade, bringing me to the realization that my miracle bypasses the natural experience, especially in consideration of the connection that I have had to caregivers, families, and survivors impacted by my life.

I never imagined anyone else feeling inspired by my story. I had never even considered speaking about my near-death experience and the hardships that I have encountered. I admit that I have been humbled by the process of creating such a vulnerable piece. Once I understood the lens of what other people saw from my experiences, my perspective became more enlightened, which is when a switch went off in my mind with relief. I have come to discover, understand, and express myself in such a way that I hope will relate to my readers.

This memoir is the literary realization of Ethan A. Poetic. It is my deepest and sincerest hope to bridge the gap, you, the reader, can be touched imperceptibly or dramatically by the true beauty of a living hero story. Hopefully, through my example, you will find a greater understanding of importance of the dedication to follow your own path and live with a purpose. The chronicles of my memoir involves adversities, education, sports, relationships, and resiliency.

Chapter 1. My up-bringing was in a single parent household.

I was born out of wedlock on a hot day at Brandywine Hospital of Caln Township, Pa on Saturday, May 23rd, 1987, and I was given the name Ethan after my mom's childhood friend, Ethan Trowery. Though I would not meet my namesake for nearly 30 years. It was just me, my mom Dorsey, and my older brother Randy. Dorsey and Arnold Armstrong never actually dated. It was simply a situation of two adults having unprotected sex, just a one-night kind of thing, but Dorsey knew right away who the father was.

She eventually told my grandparents, the late William Chase Vaughn and Alberta Charlotte Marshall-Vaughn. I can only imagine how they took the news; I am guessing they were pretty shocked, but ready to welcome me as their grandchild.

Dorsey never told me if Arnold knew she was pregnant at the time. But after I was born, several people in the community told my dad in no uncertain terms, “You have a son and his name is Ethan”.

Well, soon after my birth, Alberta and one of my aunt’s named Missy were at the Coatesville Laundromat on 3rd avenue and, by coincidence, Arnold happened to be there too. Alberta told Arnold that I was born and that he needed to see me. Unfortunately, Arnold denied me before he ever even came to see me, simply because he refused to believe the news was true.

Arnold insisted that my real dad must have been someone else and that he would not believe the rumors unless a DNA test could prove me to be his son. Eventually, something changed his mind and he agreed to meet up with Dorsey to see her baby. As soon as he saw me the truth was undeniable. We shared the same color eyes and facial features. In that moment, Arnold lost all doubt that I was his son.

It took Arnold about a month to sign the birth certificate to gain parental rights. In that time, Dorsey filed and got approved for a child support order through Chester County Domestic Relations. Once those papers were filed, the determination of my custody was in the hands of Chester County Domestic Relations. Ultimately my parents settled on co-parenting.

As I mentioned before, my name Ethan comes from Ethan Trowery. Although my mother Dorsey introduced him to me when I was a newborn, I had no recollection of this memory. Fast forward to June 19th, 2016, I became curious about the man I was names after. I had heard many things about him over the years and I developed a strong curiosity of him.

A quick Facebook search later, I found his profile and sent him a message, asking if he would be willing to meet with me. He graciously responded right away and we set a date to meet in person in Coatesville.

The day of our meeting, I was filled with excitement, wondering if this really could be the man that I was named after. I also questioned why it took this long for us to finally be reunited. Once I parked outside his home, I called him and asked him to come outside. There he was, standing in front of me in a clean, white-collar shirt and dress pants. We went to Chili's and both ordered wings, fries, and soda off the menu.

I just sat there and stared at him for a minute, but as we started eating and talking, it turned out he was just as curious about me as I was about him. We connected right away with natural energy and chemistry. I discovered he had adult children, had become a proud grandfather, and he had even graduated from Coatesville Area Senior High School, back in the day.

The funny thing was that he called his mom while we were in the restaurant and told her who I was, explaining that I had been named after him. She told us that she had found the name "Ethan" in the Bible.

That was a day I will never forget. I am proud to be named after Ethan Trowery. He may not be my biological father, but he remains very supportive, active, and present in my life.

What I have learned throughout life is that, many times, family connections created by unplanned pregnancies struggle with the same problems.

First, there is usually a failure to co-parent due to a lack of effective communication. But it is important to remember that failures are lessons meant to be learned.

Second, the parents fail to take ownership of their mistakes. Learning from failure takes humility and exploring oneself to the inner core. One can experience the true meaning of absolute liberation through the acceptance of their mistakes.

Finally, responsibility to act is not taken on an individual level. One must start a new path to create a gateway to move forward.

Cut: "But back to my story"

I did not know what life was like in other families when I was a child. Growing up, my life seemed normal because it was all that I was exposed to. In the beginning, I had three brothers living with me in the same household. We ate together at the dinner table, took turns playing video games, and watched TV together. When I look back, I realize that things changed drastically over time. Once my mom had me and my two younger brothers, my older brother received far less attention, causing him to feel neglected.

I have several more siblings. It's a mixture of some having different fathers and different mothers. Dorsey had five children through several different men, while Arnold had four children by three different women. My oldest brother Randy was nine years older than me. The next two brothers Ricky, and Ronald after me were at least a few years younger.

Prior to me being born, things did not work out with Randy's father and my mom after they dated for some time. My mother and my father never dated. But once my mom met a man named Reggie of my two younger brothers, they began to date and moved in together, making him my first stepfather. I was a toddler at the time that Randy and I were introduced to him, but my older brother got along with him instantly.

I lived in the Brandywine homes neighborhood and was completely unaware of any other siblings that I had at that point. But it turned out that Arnold had two other children with another woman, a boy named Anthony and a girl named Mercedes. Anthony was a few years older than me, while Mercedes was only two months younger than me.

With their mother Beth, Anthony. and Mercedes lived in Philadelphia, Pa. I only saw them at family gatherings through my dad or other family members from his side.

The first time I met my brother Anthony. He was in the car with our dad. They were driving through my neighborhood while I was sitting in front of my mom's house. Arnold pulled his green coupe up slowly and got out. He brought Anthony up to me and explained that I was his younger brother. I was too young to understand how I had a different older brother than lived very far away from me. But that did not stop me from having fun with Anthony. We played video games, football, basketball, watched TV, and raced each other.

Other than those short visits, I did not grow up close to Anthony. and Mercedes. Our mothers did not know each other and the distance between Philadelphia and Coatesville proved to be a barrier in our relationship. Unfortunately, our father never attempted to break this barrier to improve our relationship.

Even in adulthood, it was difficult to remain connected to my siblings. When Mercedes was pregnant with her first child, I missed the baby shower due to work conflicts. It was not until my 20th birthday that I met my niece Leah.

My birthday had never been celebrated before so this was already a special day for me. My Aunt Missy hosted the party in my grandmother's home.

But prior to the party, Arnold and my stepmom Hannah offered to take me out to go shopping for clothes, go out to eat, and give me a birthday card with money. They even brought along my younger brother, Cameron, and our cousin Paige. We all laughed together and enjoyed the time of fellowship. This would be the one and only time my dad celebrated my birthday. He did not attend the party due to prior arrangements with Cameron.

On the day of my party, I arrived to plenty of people in attendance, sharing food, sodas, gifts, cake, and ice cream. But the most special guest in attendance was my niece Leah. My two siblings from Philadelphia arrived with her and when Mercedes placed her in my arms, I was amazed by the feeling that overcame me. I felt as if I were holding my own daughter. Leah looked at me with her eyes wide open, with an essence of pure comfort. She trusted me.

The end of the party was marked by the singing of the birthday song with a cake. As the lit candles flickered and the people surrounding me sang so proudly, I felt like an innocent boy. This was the first time that I had ever experienced such a purifying feeling. I made a wish as I blew out the candles, which was followed with clapping and cheers. It was the perfect ending to a perfect day.

The two neighborhoods that I lived in were called Brandywine Homes and Oak Street. While I was living in the Brandywine Homes neighborhood, I lived across the street from some family members and close to the playground. Right up the street was a Dairy Queen, The Coatesville Area High School Campus, Laundry mat, a bank, car dealership, and the shopping center.

The home on 18 Oak Street was on top of a hill and I remember that my neighbors were very respectful to everyone. The neighborhood kids played everything together, all day and night - sports, tag, jump rope, limbo, laser tag, and video games. I vividly remember the positive men living in this neighborhood to providing for their families. They truly lived up to helping lead the strong household leader.

I was in day care and Pre-K with several kids that became my future classmates. I would attend Caln Elementary School and Gordon Middle School with a few of them. Being in the same classroom, we took turns being the class clown and enjoyed recess together either on a blacktop playground or basketball court.

Our family moved to 18 Oak Street when I was going into First grade. I remember Mrs. Susan Ross my learning support teacher visited my home with Dorsey, and other adults to discuss my performance in school.

Mrs. Ross made my experience in elementary school a pleasant one, by helping me become a better student, while creating a welcoming and encouraging environment for me. My placement in learning support was due to my struggle with reading and the neglect of my vision. Dorsey never took me to an eye doctor to get a prescription to aid my vision. It did not help that my father was also never present at any of my parent-teacher conferences or IEP meetings. Instead, Dorsey was left to figure out how to manage all of my needs on her own.

Mrs. Wilson the Art Teacher helped students with their creative side to create art works. She allowed the class to think outside the box and use our imagination. Several of the special teachers such as, music, gym, librarians, were very good with communicating with students, made sure we were held accountable for our actions, and maintained a safe environment.

One day when I came home from school, my stepfather Reggie had packed his bags and was ready to walk out the door. Things were no longer working between Reggie and Dorsey, leaving her to be a single parent again. Without a male figure leading our household anymore, my older brother took a job at McDonald's as a teenager to help provide for the family.

One day my mom introduced a man to me and my siblings inside the home. He would later become my second step dad John. He worked in the nursing field to earn money and provide for our family. He and Dorsey were dating for several years and he did tell us about the children that he had from previous relationships.

During the summer of 1997, as I came back home from playing outside, I noticed my mom had a bump showing. It turns out she was pregnant with my baby sister, Nancy. In August 1998, she was born during my sixth-grade year. One year later in June 1999, my step mom Hannah gave birth to Cameron. While Nancy lived with us at my mom's house, Cameron lived in a different home with Arnold and Hannah.

I remember the day Nancy was born like it was yesterday. She, too, was born at Brandywine Hospital. On that day she looked so innocent, small, and cute for a newborn. Packed in the room sat me, my brothers, and our stepdad John, all full of joy. The day was full of excitement and pure happiness. Unfortunately, this feeling did not last long. After the birth of Nancy, our household took a turn for the worse with Dorsey and John.

John had gone to Philadelphia, Pa on a drug and alcohol binge right after Nancy was born. Dorsey fell for the same jail talk stories countless times and ended up falling in love with John. He went on to relapse countless times, ending up in rehab, hospitals, and several county jails. I never understood how he was allowed to come back into our home with open arms and no consequences or boundaries set by Dorsey. It was at this point in my life that I began to realize that when you love a person for the wrong reasons you either start to overlook their negative behaviors, or become an enabler, rewarding their toxic behaviors.

If there was ever any suspicion of me behaving poorly, my mom threatened to send me to live with my dad. After a while, this pattern got old. I realized that she was simply playing mind games and trying to control me mentally. I began to question why our stepdad got away with so much, especially since my siblings and I were exposed to so many negative choices by her and John.

One day, Dorsey and John got into a big argument. After their words were shared, Dorsey told me and Randy to gather up John's belongings and put them all outside. As we started to do the dirty work, we noticed that he was getting quiet as he watched the whole thing take place. The following day, Dorsey allowed him right back into the house like nothing happened. I was shocked and almost could not believe what I was witnessing. There was no accountability or change between either of them.

Despite the constant strife, Dorsey and John decided to get married, with their service being held at a church. Right before the ceremony began, my uncle Jay asked me to walk up the aisle to hand the pastor the Bible. I was completely shocked by this responsibility, but the person to which the job was originally assigned backed out at the last minute. So, there I stood beside the groomsmen, the best man, and my soon-to-be official stepdad John.

After the ceremony, people started leaving to head over to the reception. I clearly remember the music on the playlist at the reception. It was full of Mint Condition, Whitney Houston, Sade, Heatwave, Earth, Wind, and Fire, and many other musical artists. We watched as Dorsey and John cut the vanilla cake that was smothered in cream frosting. Dorsey also hosted the bouquet toss, which she flung into a group of single women, following traditional wedding practices.

The old tale is that the woman who catches the bouquet would find the man of her dreams at the wedding, as the bride wished the single lady's luck in finding love. If the woman does not find the man at the wedding reception, at least she has the opportunity to go home with a very gorgeous floral centerpiece to boast about.

Meanwhile, the groom tosses the bride's garter into a crowd of single gentlemen. They fight over it with open hands and even get into contests to see who can jump the highest to catch it. The gentleman who catches it must then put it on the leg of the woman who caught the bouquet.

Once the man and woman were determined, the woman was placed in a chair in the middle of the room. The man got on one knee and pulled the garter past her foot and around her ankle. Then, as he slowly guided it up her leg, the woman began to blush immensely, until he eventually stopped once his hands get under her dress and near her thigh.

As all of this took place, I noticed just about everybody was laughing really hard with their mouths covered by their hands, cheering the man up as he made all of his slow movements up the woman's leg. I do not know if everyone in the crowd was excited for the man or purely anxious for the woman. It may have even been a combination of the two feelings. One of the women in the crowd even shouted, "Don't you worry girl, you're in good hands tonight". My guess is that that woman had a little too much champagne that night.

The purpose of a marriage is for two people to come together in unity coveted under God. Premarital counseling is usually recommended before entering this big transition.

Dorsey and John marriage did not have the right foundation. Having a marriage license, wedding ring, a ceremony, and reception do not change who the people getting married truly are. In fact, there should be time invested in preparing for married life. Watching Dorsey's marriage was a clear example for me of why it is so important to take the time to participate in pre-marital counseling to air out everything that needs to come to light. Secrets, mental health, previous sexual partners, STD status, and many other issues should be discussed prior to the union between two in marriage. But too many people have this fairytale idea of getting married and expected a Disney story without doing any of the work ahead of time to create a healthy relationship.

News flash: There is a big difference between fantasy, entertainment and reality. Whatever behavior patterns, whether they be healthy or unhealthy, will be carried into the marriage, which usually leads to divorce or celebrating each anniversary together.

Fast forward several years later, once those papers were signed, my mom finally divorced John for good. I'll talked more about moving to Lancaster, Pa later on.

He never gave us a farewell speech or made any big gestures. He simply moved out and took his negative behaviors with him, which alleviated much of the stress and chaos in our home. I no longer had to worry about random arguments lasting all hours of the nights, or the countless calls to the police for domestic violence.

The process of going through a divorce does break up the family. It can be for the better or for the worst. I know once a divorce is finalized with a divorce decree order from the Lancaster County Courthouse, new problems and challenges arise if the situation involves a child. The child may be forced to choose which parent to live with in family court. However, if there are no children involved, both parties get to start a new journey in their lives with less complications and an easier transition.

The nightmare was over, and Dorsey was back to being a single parent all over again. Growing up, I did not understand why people would do drugs. I was confused as to why a single mother would even expose her children to such negativity.

There comes a significant cost for allowing children to see an addict self-medicate and submerge in deep underlying pain, wounds, and scars. The world sees very few children brave enough to go against the grain, while the others give into what they experience at home. As these children grow up around the world, they will often feel the effects of the harmful damage and have severe consequences in their own lives.

As I reflect on all of the addiction that I was exposed to in my lifetime, I understand now that many people have flashbacks of memories, suppressed trauma, or unresolved wounds. Therefore, addicts turn to drugs, alcoholism, other substances, or anything that will numb the mind for a moment. The short-term high messes up the natural chemical balance in exchange for brief happiness and "feel good" chemicals. These chemicals interact with the neurotransmitters that affect the mood, such as serotonin, oxytocin, endorphins, and dopamine.

One of the reasons why people turn to drugs, even in the recreational sense, it to cope with the underlying pain that they have connected to their childhood memories. Whether that be because they were not held or properly protected as a child or supported as a teenager to hold them up on solid ground, resulting in a turn to drugs for a false salvation and false sense of happiness, causing many setbacks in their lives.

The situation will only become worse as the addict starts developing an addiction that becomes a stronghold. The addicts will steal, guilt trip, swindle, manipulate, and pawn anything that they can get their hands on.

While addicts harm the people that are the closest to them the most, I have heard of stories that involved family members cutting off the addicts and disowning them for a more peaceful life.

The old saying is that the people you are around the most are who you are likely to become. Another old saying is show me your friends, and I will show you your future.

Nobody should put up with those negative consequences and feel the effects of somebody else's deadly choices unless they choose to give into a downward spiral and dig themselves deeper into a grave. That's why keeping a distant relationship is a new boundary to be taken on a priority level.

The emotional foundation of an addict is very fragile and broken. It will not withstand the tests of time and all life's challenges. It is certainly no fun living life in a dark place, bringing down the people that love and care about you dearly. Before you know it, those people stop answering phone calls, emails, texts, and listening to the sob stories. They will become fed up with the chaos and cut ties.

There are case studies of those addicted to prescription medicine have shown an increased rate of fraud, families being broken up, newborn babies hooked on drugs and people being sentenced to lengthy jail terms. Law enforcement created a budget for the Task Force, and people's lives forever changed as certain neighborhoods and communities turned into war zones.

Families can be rebuilt through family court, a social worker, setting new boundaries, and giving an ultimatum for rehab or teen challenges directly related to the addict. Sometimes they must be broken up when you have no choice but to distance yourself from an abusive situation. Either way, a series of decisions that has to be made for better or worse. You have to be intentional about your demands and starting new behavior patterns.

There are millions of children across the world living their lives without their biological fathers and mothers. The stories being told can be life changing as the void is in the children's mind. The domino effects impact their personal growth, identity, and development. Having both biological parents in the child's life is to truly take care of the child, starting with providing a strong foundation, stability, resources, self-worth, courage, and confidence.

There are some children that are placed in foster care and adopted to be in a better or more harmful environment. Sometimes those environments have mixed results depending on what is provided and invested into the children. The children may have a hard time finding their identity, knowing their biological family, family history, or having proper closure.

Growing up, playing video games was my hobby. I played against my older brothers, family members, and neighborhood friends. Most of the losses came against my older brothers since they were more experienced than I was at the time.

During my early childhood, my Aunt Belinda bought me and my siblings our first Sega Genesis for Christmas. I remember unwrapping the wrapping paper off the big box. As soon as I realized it was a video game system, I was ready to play. I observed my older brother navigate the setup of the system with the tv, hooking up all of the cords to their proper inputs.

As he became more comfortable with the game, he began to invite his friends over to play with him. I watched them with admiration of how they were so capable of being competitive and friendly at the same time. Once it was my turn to play against somebody, I usually lost, taking it to the chin without any hard feelings, and focused on getting better with each game. Once I got older, things began to turn in my favor and I started a winning streak against the older people in my life.

At my relatives' homes, they each had the same game system as well. Several years later, my other aunts Tancy and Winter bought more game systems, such as PlayStation, PlayStation 2, Xbox, and Xbox 360. Playing video games was an outlet for me. It kept me out of trouble and helped me channel my emotions, to avoid some of my underlying pain, instead focusing on my moments where I was able to shine. Little did I know, playing video games would allow me to learn about football and basketball.

Football became my biggest interest. I played it in real life at the gym, parks, neighborhood, and watched it on TV. Barry Sanders was a running back for the Detroit Lions. I could relate to him for being smaller in height, which led to my desire of playing running back.

I was not concerned about playing defense, and I never had a football idol on the defensive side. It was not until I saw Deion Sanders, aka Prime Time, with his flashy moves as a cornerback and punt return, man! He had that It factor on the football field with style, as he usually locked down his side of the field or the best receivers of the other team. I liked what I saw and knew I needed to step up my defensive skills right away. I used to practice a tackling drill where I wrapped up the person I was against, and I found this to be very simple. There was also a back-peddle drill with cones that I used to work on my agility and took more time to master. I learned that a person needs to have a strong hip flexor to turn or rotate on sudden movements.

I remember listening to the sports commentators John Madden, Tony Dungy, and many more. They seemed to speak a language I understood completely without a translator. My football IQ was naturally incomparable

---

Back to my early childhood, I had just finished 5th grade and the ceremony for my promotion was at Caln Elementary School. My cousin Becky had her parents there to support her, but neither one of my parents were present at that moment. September of 1998 my 6th grade year at Gordon Middle School, Dorsey told me that I would now start living with Arnold and Hannah. They did not even ask for my opinion or feedback on how I felt about moving away.

I was heading into 6th grade, and Arnold decided to sign me up for Midget League Football, playing for the Coatesville Red Raiders. I was now living at my dad's home, and my life was very different being away from the city of Coatesville, Pa. For the first time, my biological dad was more active and present in my life. That was a new feeling in my soul as I was in transition to a new life and 6th grade.

The time I spent with Arnold and Hannah showed me a different perspective. There was plenty of food, soft beverages, and snacks inside the cabinets, refrigerator, and kitchen closet. The neighborhood was a roundabout, very exclusive, with fewer neighbors, and large land to do anything you wanted on. There was more privacy with a big garage, blacktop driveway, and several rooms inside the brand-new home. Although I was surrounded by my dad and the life he created, I felt lonely because I was more used to living with several of my siblings, seeing my childhood friends in the neighborhood, and having more freedom to visit my family members.

Living in the suburbs of Sadsburyville, Pa was far away from family members, friends, and middle school. Early in the morning Hannah would drop me off in Coatesville at my Aunt Stacey's home and walk one block to Gordon Middle School.

Arnold and Hannah were living in a different school zone. Therefore, I was supposed to catch a bus to be attending South Brandywine Middle. The truth is my mom never filled out the paper for me to transfer to South Brandywine Middle School. Dorsey still had me enrolled at Gordon Middle School since she had full custody.

I did not know anything about transferring rules, school zones, and changing mailing addresses. I just knew there was a verbal agreement between my parents, and that mistake proved very costly later on down the road.

Once again, they ended up failing to co-parent for my best interest as they always did. I had been to South Brandywine Middle School beforehand for a couple of wrestling meets during my 7th and 8th grade year at Gordon Middle School. The South Brandywine Middle School was very different from a city middle school. It was a wide-open space with more land, trees, and other elements of nature.

Seeing that my dad actually cared, especially through his actions, gave me a new sense of reality. Yet, looking back on my childhood, the foundation was still fragile and broken. It does not matter how much money you earn, the type of car you drive, or the nice clothes or sneakers you wear. If your relationship with a biological parent is not on the right path or there is a lack of proper communication, there will be challenges that will come up, and it is only a matter of time before a fall out takes place.

Things took a turn for the worst right before one of my football games on a Sunday afternoon at Scott Field. My late grandmother June E. Smith had informed Dorsey that my Arnold was filing for full custody through Domestic Relations and a motion to remove child support.

My dad had breached a verbal agreement with my mom. As my football game ended, Dorsey and Arnold got into a big shouting match, and I was caught in the middle. I was not sure what was going on besides hearing loud voices. No child deserves to be caught in the middle of chaos between two parents.

They should be looking out for the best interest and wellbeing of the child. Until the actual work is done between the biological parents, the relationship will keep failing with a capital F. Parents have to look at themselves in the mirror to take ownership of the role. They contributed to the situation, and no matter how small or big, fault is fault.

I ended up leaving with my dad after the game. While inside the car with my dad, he drove me back to my mom's home. The purpose was to pick up some sneakers. As I opened up the front door, I noticed nobody was home. I remember not having enough time to find my sneakers because my dad came running to the door telling me to get them and leave with him.

At the same time, the phone was ringing, and John on the other line told me to stay home and that my mom was on her way home. I was caught in a bad situation of choosing between staying home until my mom got there or leaving with my dad. I left with my dad since I heard his voice very loud with bass. But I was not able to find a pair of sneakers and we ended up driving to his home for dinner.

The next day at Gordon Middle School, I walked around the entire day with my football cleats and got a gym detention for not wearing the proper shoes for gym class. I was too embarrassed to tell anybody why I came to school wearing football cleats. After school, I told my dad that I was issued an after-school detention for not wearing the proper footwear. He told my Hannah to pick me up after school, and she confirmed it with me.

The following day after school, as I was meeting the gym teacher to serve my gym detention. He was very curious about why I would show up to school wearing football cleats for gym class. For all the years of being an educator in a public-school district, he had never seen a student do that before in his life at school. I told my gym teacher Mr. Smith the entire situation. Mr. Smith really felt bad for me by showing sympathy and empathy.

He ended up letting me out early because the situation was beyond my control. When I got out of detention, my friend, Terrell, told me that my mom Dorsey was looking for me. Suddenly, out of nowhere, she saw me and told me I was leaving with her. That was the turn back moment of my life since Dorsey was taking custody of me and putting her foot down.

Once me and my mom went outside to her car, my stepmom Hannah arrived at Gordon Middle School in her car, and Dorsey had a brief conversation with Hannah. Thankfully, it ended peacefully. By the time my mom and I got back inside her house, my dad was walking up the steps and he was there banging on the windows to the point that I thought they were going to break and shatter.

They got into yet another argument. Only this time the lay of the land was much different. My mom won the argument because my dad knew he was wrong for what he did and that the trust was broken. The battle was over and Dorsey won the war. This encounter led me to think of the saying, “You can’t beat a person when you’re on their turf.” After all, my mom had a home field advantage in this battle.

My dad left that day as a hurt man, making the walk of shame down the hill, and driving away in his car. I guess that moment led him to just giving up on our relationship, after going through so much stress, leading to the downfall of my relationship with him.

As I looked at my mom, it was clear that she just wanted me to finish up my homework assignments as she got prepared to take care of my other siblings. There were not any more shouting matches between my parents. Moving forward they just kept the communication to very minimal, which consisted of the annual custody hearings through Chester County Domestic Relations. I remember seeing court orders in the mail every now and then.

Both of my parents kept talking among themselves without me giving my input for my own life.

Moving forward, now that I was back living at my mother's house, my life changed yet again – I was forced to press the reset button on my young life. I was now responsible for watching over my younger siblings Ricky, Ronald and newborn baby sister Nancy, while my mom left for work on the first or second shift. I still managed to finish the midget league football season, this time without the support of my dad, mom, grand mom June, and stepmom Hannah. John was in and out of rehab with his drug addiction.

It seemed like my parents were so caught up in their chaos and differences, that they forgot to look out for me. My routine after school was pick up my Nancy from the babysitter next door, cook, and make sure my other siblings were inside the home. I felt like Nancy was my new born baby since I was playing the father role. I would end up walking, catching a ride, or riding my bike round trip from my home to football practice. The journey started on 1st avenue and 18 oak street to 9th avenue at Victor Abdala Sr. Memorial Park.

My dad John, stepmom Hannah, and grandmother June were no longer involved, and the support just ended without any discussion with me. My dad was no longer in the stands to see me or meet me after the football games were over. I saw my teammates with their family members, yet no family members of mine were there to support me. I would either walk or get dropped off at Scott Field for the football games. After the football games were over, I would either walk back home or one of my teammate's parents would drop me off at home. I really did appreciate the kindness of their hearts by looking out for me.

Honestly, I could have thrown in the white towel for my personal reasons, hardships, and lack of family support. I could have quit the football team and given up on myself. But there was still something inside of me that decided to see the football season through until the very end.

On a Saturday morning, my stepmom Hannah came to my mom's home to drop off my football equipment. I had already missed two football practices during the week since I did not have my equipment. I was also still taking care of my baby sister Nancy and two other siblings.

Once I arrived back to football practice, my two coaches asked why I missed those practices. I had told them what happened. They felt sorry for me and allowed me to show up to practice without any consequences. My teammates were very happy to see me back on the team. I felt a sense of belonging and acceptance from the football team that I did not feel with my parents.

As the football season ended, there was an all-star football game to play against a team in Ohio. I saw other players from different teams we competed against join the Coatesville Midget Football team for the all-star game. I did not sign up because my mom did not have the money as she told me. But there was a banquet to attend after the all-star game was over for me to look forward to.

The banquet was held right inside the cafeteria at Coatesville Area High School 9th and 10th grade center. I remember my uncle Jimmy giving an amazing speech at the podium that was followed with rounds of applause from the rest of the adults in the room. I even saw some of my cousins and other relatives at this banquet. But the most important thing that I remember about the banquet was the sense of community that could be felt in the room. The banquet was the highlight of acknowledging the players for their commitment towards hard work, as well as recognize the investment of the volunteer coaches, booster club members, parents, and guardians. It takes an entire community to operate a successful midget league team for any sport as a feeder program.

Looking back, I have learned that this situation was just leading me to doing more things on my own. I was learning that in my life, I would achieve greater things without the presence of my estranged dad and mom. I understand no situation is ever perfect and sometimes in life we have to make the most of opportunities that require resilience.

However, because of the effects I felt during my sixth-grade year while playing midget league football and watching my siblings, I made the decision not to play football at both Gordon middle school and Coatesville midget league football my seventh-grade year. The chaos was too much for me to handle being caught in the middle of it. It was my responsibility to find a safe haven and create my own peace.

When I chose to not play football, my 7th grade year was very different as I completed my work assignments and was a class clown sometimes. I remember seeing some of my classmates wearing the shoulder pads, knee pads, thigh pads, mouth guard, and a protective cup for their private parts. Meanwhile, I was no longer at a football practice to hear the sounds of pads hitting, whistles blowing, and the reviewing of the plays. Some of my classmates would wear the black and gold football or red and black jerseys to school on game day.

I did not sign to play football since there was the uncertainty of if my parents would embarrass me all over again. Neither one of them was willing to tell me the whole truth of what happened behind the scenes. I often wondered what really took place during their conversations without me present. Some of my classmates would ask me why I did not play football. I could not tell them the real reasons and open up about what was going on in my life.

One day I got picked up from school by my dad and he asked me why I did not sign up for midget league football or for Gordon Middle School. But I never opened up to him about it. Deep down inside I really wanted to play football again, yet I just did not feel secure within myself to do it again.

In order for me to sign up for Coatesville Red Raiders Midget League football a fee has to be paid at the time of sign up, with proof of insurance, and other paperwork signed. At Gordon Middle School, I would need my mom to fill out the physical form, providing proof of insurance card, and medical records.

I do not regret the decision of not playing football my 7th grade year. I just dislike the lack of support for my life which led to me watching football games from the sidelines. I kept my truth to myself for a long time until my adult years when I finally started speaking up about it.

I participated in wrestling my seventh-grade year at Gordon Middle School. My dad had said he used to do wrestling in both middle and high school. That influenced me to do that on my own without him. Once I came home to see my mom, I mentioned to her that I wanted to be signed up for the middle school wrestling team. As she was looking at me and reading through the paperwork, she decided to fill out the paperwork in a black ink pen and the next day I gave the paperwork to the athletic director.

The wrestling coach was Mr. Kramer and there were less than ten students signed up on the team. We were all competitive on individual levels. But we did not have enough teammates to compete with other teams with over 30 students signed up. Most of the male student-athletes at Gordon Middle School, were trying out for the basketball team or getting ready for spring track and field during the winter season. I did not compete in track and field my 7th grade year, I should have signed up for the experience

In my eight-grade year I chose to take a leap of faith by both playing football and wrestling at Gordon Middle School. After I came home from school, I went inside my mom's room to leave the paperwork on my mom's dresser for her to see after she got home from work. That told her I wanted to play football again, this time at Gordon Middle School, and she had left the paperwork in the kitchen for me to pick up. This time was much different than the last time.

I felt like I needed to play football and be part of the team. I needed to be involved in the game and practices for my own best interest. I knew ahead of time my dad was not going to be involved in me being signed up and my mom was not going to be coming to the practices or games.

As the fall 2000 season started, I was not embarrassed by my parents' absences at any of my football games or wrestling meets anymore. Since nobody ever showed up at anything or truly cared to support me, there was no chaos. I was a student-athlete while taking care of my siblings right after practice. My mom never hired a babysitter or had a man inside the home on a consistent basis.

I saw how my teammates had parents waiting for them after games to embrace them. I would have played track and field my eighth-grade year, but I was forced to move to Lancaster, PA March 4th. It was not until early April 2001 that I was enrolled at Wheatland Middle School and the deadline had passed for me to sign up to be on the track and field team.

At the time there were only two middle school track teams called southwest and southeast. The southwest team was formed by student athletes from both Wheatland Middle School and Reynolds Middle School, while the northeast team was both Lincoln Middle School and Hazel Jackson Middle School, formerly named "Edward Hand Middle School".

One day in December 2000 of a life changing moment occurred. I was headed straight home after school to begin my holiday break and arrived to find my mom in the living room. She told me that I would be spending Christmas with my dad and stepmom Hannah. They picked me up that same day and took me with them.

Later that evening, we arrived at my dad and stepmom's home with all of my sibling's present. My older brother Anthony, sister Mercedes from Philadelphia, and our baby brother Cameron were happy to see me. As I walked into the living room there were plenty of Christmas gifts inside of the family spaces. There were so many gifts it looked like somebody went on a shopping spree at Macy's, Toys R Us, Walmart, and Amazon. My eyes were lit up with hope that Christmas would be a good holiday with the family this year.

I never in my life during my childhood saw that many wrapped gifts underneath the tree with ornaments, special lights, and the gold star on top of the tree. Little did I know there was a rude awakening about to take place at the home.

The early morning on Christmas day we had family members coming over for fellowship. There was plenty of food and soft beverages being served. Once it was time to open the gifts, I saw my older brother and sister with smiles of excitement on their faces. I started looking around the Christmas tree inside of both living rooms for my gifts.

As it turns out there was not anything for me. I was confused as a kid wondering why my siblings received Christmas gifts but not me. As I started looking around there was nobody to give me an answer. My stepmom Hannah, by surprise tells me to come up the stairs with her. Meanwhile, my dad was drinking beer and the adults were playing card games and watching NFL football games.

Hannah and I went inside Cameron's room, as she went inside the closet, she pulled out a Christmas gift for me. I felt so happy that she cared about me and made sure I was not empty handed on Christmas Day. I went into a different room to put the gift away in my bookbag. Afterwards, I went back downstairs as though nobody knew about the gift I received from my stepmom. We ended up keeping a holiday secret Santa between us for several years.

Looking back now my dad was the person that did not care to buy me any Christmas gifts. I guess that is what happens when the relationship becomes estranged with a broken foundation. After that happened, I never went back to the home for Christmas again.

I did not feel appreciated or welcomed at all. I understand there are unresolved problems in the relationship between me, my dad, and my mom. But there was really no point in having me around for the Holidays, especially since I was being mistreated by my dad. He knew what he was doing the whole time as a grown man and it was truly disrespectful. Once I got dropped off back at my mom's home, I did not bother telling her anything about what happened. I may have went to my room to play video games and watch tv.

The moral of this situation is that even though I never received a Christmas Gift from my own dad for that Christmas holiday, there was somebody else who still cared enough to provide me with a Christmas gift -- my stepmom Hannah. The saying goes, "It takes a special person to help take care of and raise a child that isn't their own, both biologically, and legally." I suppose my stepmom is one of many special people around the world.

I remember when my dad and his girlfriend, now wife, were living together in a two-bedroom apartment in Downingtown, Pa. The owner was living directly across from the apartment complex and my dad would give him a check for the rent each month.

There was a time we went swimming, and as my dad was talking to the lifeguard, I made the mistake of jumping in the deep end of the pool. My dad jumped right into the pool and saved me. He was a former swimmer at Coatesville Area Senior High School, so it must have been a natural reaction to dive into the pool at a certain angle, as he grabbed me and raised me up for air.

I had not thought about that moment until I started writing this memoir. As I look back on that moment, it showed he actually did care about my life, I just do not know the underlying reasons on why he stopped caring about the relationship that we shared.

Another memory was in the spring season of my 6th grade year. My teacher went to answer the phone and told me to go directly to the main office. I knew I was not in trouble, but I did not know why I was being summoned. As I started walking closer and closer the empty hallway, I finally realized the reason. There stood my dad and stepmom Hannah. They took me outside, opened the tailgate to a red Chevy truck and revealed a brand-new bike for me. I was very happy and could not wait to ride it.

Instead of dropping me off at home, my dad took a turn onto the highway. We ended up going to a sneaker store, where my stepmom purchased a new pair of sneakers for me. The sneakers that I was wearing before that were really busted and full of holes. But they cared enough to make sure I was taken care of.

They noticed my mom was not taking care of me financially with the child support checks that were being mailed to her. The money was never in my hands. I only saw the child support checks in the mail, and my mom Dorsey was in charge of it. As I got dropped off home, I walked inside to find my mom sleeping in her room. I told her about the new bike my dad and stepmom gave me. She was excited for me, and she noticed my new sneakers as well. For the rest of the school year, I did not have to worry about wearing those over used sneakers anymore.

There's plenty of things I really disliked about my dad. He was always starting something between me, my siblings, and cousins. Whether it was starting instigating a fight over the front seat, playing a sport, or name calling behind somebody's back. He never asked what I wanted to do, how I felt about certain things, and did not allow me to have my own identity. That was truly the beginning of what was starting to drive a big wedge between me and my dad over the years. It really stopped once I saw him less and less. The relationship has become estranged since then.

I believe that type of negative influence had me acting out for attention, by trying to fill in the voids in my own life. Those missing voids were words of affirmation, effective communication, acceptance, and having a balanced relationship.

There was a time as a teenager I wanted to grow my hair to be braided.

I refused to get my haircut in front of everybody at the barber shop, resulting in my mom being very pissed off. We left and she let me have it on the car ride home, yelling at me and lecturing me about the scene that I made. She tried to call my dad to tell him everything, but he did not answer to respond to her. My mom called my aunt Missy and uncle Daryl, and they were really upset with me.

I ended up being dropped off at my aunt Maggie's home for the weekend because my mom was so upset. I was having a good time hanging out with my cousins and visiting other family members. We had ordered Americanized Chinese food, drank soft beverages, and played video games at their home on 5th avenue. I felt like I was enjoying the time because I was proud of myself for standing up for myself, my identity, and expression. As I look back now, there was a lot of unresolved underlying pain that was passed on to me by my parents. They never were planning on having that heart to heart talk with me about the way things never worked out with them.

The feeling was relieved to express myself and have my own identity.

Moving forward, one day me and my mom got into a big argument over me refusing to get my haircut again. This time my dad could not do anything besides say I have to wait until I turn 18. Several years later, once I turned 18, I started growing my hair into an afro, and I found a woman to braid my hair for the very first time.

While attending Wheatland Middle School, I remember getting on the bus along with several students taking a tour of the high school.

The J.P McCaskey High School experience was a breath of fresh air. I still remember my tour guide. He was playing varsity football and track. I remember being inside both of McCaskey West and McCaskey East buildings. The West building had been there for over sixty years and the East building was still new.

The student population growth created the need for McCaskey to build an east building. Moving forward, the school board members had to be creative with the school district of Lancaster's budget to find the overhead cost to hire more certified teachers, support staff, café staff, and maintenance men.

I was originally supposed to be at McCaskey East my freshman year, but I was one of several students placed at the Ramada Inn Hotel. I remember having classrooms inside the conference rooms. Due to the renovations at the McCaskey East Building, all freshman and sophomores were placed at smaller buildings around the city of Lancaster. I did not have a chance to enjoy the campus environment until my eleventh-grade year. The school buses would pick up students at the small learning communities and drop them off at the high school campus.

Chapter 2. Men Leaving Me

My first stepdad Ricky entered my life when I was a toddler. He lived with the family, as in cohabitating with my mom. I spent more time with him than I did with my own biological dad Arnold in the early years of my childhood. Looking back, in order for my dad to see me in person, he and my mom Dorsey had to communicate together. Sometimes I got dropped off at my aunt's Joan's home or my grandmother June's home, and I was later picked up by a family member on my dad's side.

My mom told me my dad would say he was coming to pick me up and would not do it. I still do not know the whole truth. The truth always seemed to be withheld from me. But the writing was on the wall for a failed relationship between me and my dad. As for my stepdad Ricky, I just know he was present inside the household, worked consistently, and contributed to the household. Once he left the family, I saw him less and less overtime. Many years later down the road he did give me an explanation on why the relationship with my mom didn't work out.

I was very lost and confused about this change. All I knew was that he and my mom were no longer together. But since they had two kids together, there was still a need to co-parent together. My mom was now a single woman raising four boys on her own.

This left a void in the lives of me and my brothers. The conflicting relationship between my mom and stepdad Ricky was never addressed and the solution was not a positive one. Society tends to question single parent households without noticing a breakdown must have happened to cause the divide. Over the next few years, my mom had to take on the sole responsibility of leading a household full of young boys.

The next man to enter my life was my mom's boyfriend Jack. He never lived with use in the house, but he would visit a lot to spend time with us and play video games. Then a break-up between my mom and Jack and they remained friends. The next man my mom started dating was a long-distance boyfriend and I saw him maybe three times. After a while, he stopped showing up so there must have been another breakup. After that, my mom dated another man. Although this man had a son who I had the chance to meet, his breakup with my mom did not impact my life. Business continued as usual.

I have come to realize that the more children a single parent has, regardless of if it is a man or a woman, the dating field becomes a greater challenge, and their dating value may decrease. For any child to see a pattern of men leaving a household, the effects can influence personalities, mindsets, and the development of a pattern of inconsistencies. Every man or woman has their reason for leaving or abandonment. The hole left in a child's heart leaves unanswered questions being swept under the rug. A child does deserve to know their identity to move forward in their own life.

The court system will hold a boyfriend or the man that is cohabitating with a woman accountable to pay child support, even though the child is not his, legally or through DNA. There have even been situations when a woman gave a false name of a man on a birth certificate. A man has to go through so many court battles to avoid paying child support and have justice on his side. To find the whole truth should be very simple and straightforward to give closure for everyone involved, but it is never that simple.

A man can question a woman before marrying her, asking why things did not work out between her and the father of her children. The same can be said vice versa against men as well. In my situation, my experience with my dad and my stepdads was an unhealthy one. There was a high likelihood of me repeating the cycle that was shown to me through their example.

I had some work to do with going from the victim to victor mindset. There simply were no father-son moments, pictures, or rite of passage rituals in my life. The foundation I was standing on as a kid did not have stability, which led to me having a victim mindset until I made the choice to become a victor. That statement I wrote took humility to admit even though my circumstances were not my fault. It was purely the result of choices made by the closest adults in my life.

I once carried the burden of my parents' mistakes, much like many other children and adults around the world. My experience was life changing and the cost was that heavy burden that I was never meant to carry.

The mark has been missed by the parents for not taking ownership and changing the behavior pattern. Now we see why the family services, domestic relations, social workers, and children youth services are overworked and backlogged.

Once the adults come to break the cycle and not allow future generations to carry unnecessary burdens, they allow future generations to live in freedom, with less delays, and chaos.

I remember a police officer coming into my classroom at Caln Elementary School. He spoke about the D.A.R.E program and the consequences people paid for using drugs, alcohol, and other harmful substances. Little did I know, as a kid I would have a negative stepdad come into my life with a lot of excess baggage. Once my previous stepdad Ricky left the household and a series of break-ups my mom had with other men. Our family was living in poverty inside the household.

May you imagine every month being on Section 8, food stamps, and other government assistant programs? Completing the annual paperwork for updates on household changes, increase or decrease with working wages, somebody leaving or moving in. Those things I mentioned were intended to help people get back on their feet and eventually transition off of them to be more independent and self-sufficient.

Yet the government programs were used to enable women of color and take men of color out of the household. The government knew how to capitalize on some young minds that did not see the full picture or the fine print.

This leaks into the world of education through the targeting people of color/minorities for learning support classes. The public education system was setup to inhibit minorities/people of color from growing and fully blossoming. By placing some minority students in learning support classes, they have even more barriers to overcome, and they become limited to boxed up surroundings. They are not allowed to be fully unleashed to make the most of their childhood like they would in a general education classroom.

While non-minority women can have a man living inside the home and further their education, the government was sending two different messages to the public, which led to mixed results and consequences for the future generations. As we can see more often based on the data and USA federal census reports, there are plenty of single parent households of made up of minority men or women

Every adult parent has a story to tell about why they are still a single parent or suffering in silence with family secrets. From not making better choices, counseling, and join a mentorship program. There are some comeback stories of single parent households breaking the negative cycle and creating their own narrative.

As for my own experience in a single parent household, my parents were never together, and my mom was a single parent of four boys. There was another child born several years later. I was never told about the situation as a child or teenager. By the time I was in 4th grade a man got introduced to me and my siblings. I thought nothing of it until John started living with us. This time my mom stayed with him until she filed for divorce several years later.

By that time, I was a teenager and no longer playing sports at J.P. McCaskey High School. My step dad John worked, paid bills, and took the family out to eat. But he had a very dark side of being drunk and high from drug binges. He would leave for Philadelphia for weeks and several months at a time. I knew what was going on and my mom Dorsey allowed him to come back without any consequences.

Dorsey cannot play the victim and be the head of the household. She allowed me and my siblings Randy, Ricky, Ronald, and Nancy, to be around negative influences and there was no protection against being exposed to it. I had to call the cops due to domestic violence, and sometimes the cops showed up to the home to serve a warrant for arrest, such as missed court dates, unpaid parking tickets, not making payments on court costs, and fines.

One time, the cops showed up, approaching both the front and back doors. I allowed them in as they searched for my John and Dorsey. This experience was normal to me, but I did not like it at all. The cops were showing up for the bad choices the adults made with no regard, while me and my siblings felt the effects.

I remember coming home from Gordon Middle School to all the doors and windows locked. Normally an adult is home to let me and my siblings inside. That day me and my siblings went to eat some food and went directly to our grandmother's home. She and my aunt Lee were surprised to see me and Ricky. Later that evening the phone rang. My grandmother answered and my mom was on the line saying to meet at her best friend's home. Upon arrival, Chinese food was ordered for dinner. Once we got back home, I realized my stepdad John went on another drug binge.

It was a sad period to go through during my 7th grade year of middle school. I still managed to compete in the wrestling program without any support from my parents or stepdad John. Their marriage was not a healthy model to follow at all. Going to church or moving to Lancaster did not to create a better environment.

The divorce ended the chaos with a lasting negative effect, leading to addressing or suppressing new or old problems. The drug situation was gone but it left the relationship between me and my mom Dorsey really damaged to the point of arguments. I remember hearing threats of sending me to my dad, yet I knew she was not going to do that since they did not trust each other. Outside of paying child support he was barely involved in my life as is.

Chapter 3. Lancaster, PA

I had just finished two successful sports seasons in both football and wrestling in Coatesville. Our football team at Gordon Middle School was composed of an elite group of playmakers. We had a combination of speed, power, and quick big men. Our two coaches, Coach Hovis and Coach Keech, were blessed to coach such a special group of young men. There were no favorites as we played for the best interest of the team.

Our 8th grade team usually blew teams out with the mercy rule going into effect. The offense was a Wing-T formation emphasizing on finishing the blocks, playing until the whistle blew, and we averaged over 5 touchdowns per game. The defense was a base 4-3 and nickel package since there was team speed at the skills positions. Our dominant linemen sometimes were double teamed, and we created turnovers into points.

The team was a very special group of young men playing together with a lot of chemistry. We lived in the same school zone for several years. Our families grew up together and held up the tradition of being positive student-athletes.

We stayed humble throughout the season and went undefeated. I remember the middle school news article stating most of us projected to start Varsity Football by our 10th grade year. The future of our football program was looking very bright and full of great promise ahead. A professional photographer even took our team photo for the daily local newspaper.

As a wrestler I had some individual success, I was named the team captain, and continued to get better as the season went along. Late February of 2001, I went to sign up for the co-ed track team and our team was expecting to go undefeated, win several gold medals, and maybe compete on the freshmen team. Once again, things took a different turn when my mom told me that we will be leaving Coatesville to move to Lancaster, PA.

I did not want to leave my childhood friends, family, and everything I knew behind. In my mind, nothing was ever going to be the same and, once again, I had no say in the matter. The day I told my classmates and teammates everything, it felt as if I was going on with my life without them. I truly did not want to move away to start all over. I wanted to finish what we started as student-athletes.

The community of Coatesville had faith that we were going to win the Ches-Mont, District and PIAA championships in high school. We were going to learn the ropes from the upperclassmen, coaches, and trainers. The talent, experience, grit, and determination were there in our special group of athletes.

On my last day at Gordon Middle School, it just felt sad for me, knowing that I may not see my friends, teammates, or teachers again. That last day just was not the same as it normally would be on a regular school day. I remember the art teacher gave me a better grade for my fresh start at a new middle school. That was very kind hearted of him to do for me.

The lunchroom felt like my last supper since there was no turning back after that day. Once the final bell dismissed the students from school, I took everything out of my locker and put it into my book bag. As I started leaving, people were wishing me good luck, shaking hands, and we all started walking home.

Once my life began to start over in Lancaster, the environment was totally different in comparison to living in the city of Coatesville and Caln Township.

My family and I arrived in Sterling Place and a new chapter was in the making for my life. The new room with closet space was right next to the kitchen, living room, and the small side bathroom. I felt a breath of fresh air as I looked outside to see plenty of trees, green grass, red fire hydrants, townhouses, and apartments.

Our family moved Sunday March 4th, 2001. I did not know anyone in Sterling Place, but word of mouth started to travel fast about me and my family moving in. I was supposed to attend Wheatland Middle School within a week. I had to stay home from middle school for the first twenty-one days since the transfer forms were delayed and something went wrong with the enrollment. I did not end up starting at Wheatland middle school until Monday April 2nd, 2001.

While Ricky and Ronald had already started elementary school, I was at home watching my younger sister Nancy. We enjoyed each other's company most of the time.

My experiences at Wheatland Middle School were very different as I look back. I saw more Puerto Rican students in the hallways, gym class, and classrooms. Before then, I was more used to seeing African Americans, Europeans, and a few people of other ethnicities. I heard so many Spanish conversations that did not even relate to me since I did not understand the Spanish language.

The cafeteria was full of diversity as students of different shades of skin colors got along and fellowshipped together. The principals were always present throughout the day while school was in session. They walked with authority that commanded the utmost respect. The playground was a mixture of a parking lot, basketball courts, open grass on the football field, and a tree.

There weren't any serious bullying problems going on since there was a uniform policy in effect at Wheatland Middle School. I went from choosing my own clothing to wear at Gordon Middle School to following a dress code at Wheatland Middle School. In fact, they were the first middle to have a dress code policy approved by the School Board of Lancaster.

Wheatland Middle School is located in Lancaster Township. The school zone is directly across from the Lancaster city line. Students from both Lancaster City and Lancaster Township attended Wheatland Middle School on the Southwest side.

Starting a new school was a big adjustment. Nobody knew who I was, and I was just labeled the new kid with a lot of hype. My first class was art and the art teacher introduced me in front of everybody. Some nice girls sat next to me and introduced themselves to me. They asked me if I needed help with our class assignment to help me with creating a folder, choosing the colors, measuring with a ruler, and creating the design. The girls sure did know how to welcome me with open arms with no hidden agendas. They were genuine throughout the spring of 2001. I never experienced this type of attention from girls before in my life.

Being naïve to this was a learning curve since nobody told me what to do with these types of attention or at least show me the ropes about the opposite sex or gender in great detail. I was either learning on my own or through small conversations with my peers.

I soon saw teenage girls pregnant with their bellies showing as their lives were forever changed. I saw boys working at fast food restaurants earning money just to take care of their babies and their girlfriends. I thought condoms and birth control were supposed to prevent STDs and pregnancies.

I believe young teenagers need to think twice about having sex. Something could go wrong due to lack of knowledge, preparation, or proper guidance. Those teen parents soon realized the truth is condoms can break, tear, or not even fit right. There is no turning back the hands of time once the sperm and eggs combine together. The girl or woman has a big decision to make once she professes she's pregnant. Birth control is an entirely different world since some women use it at their own choice and risk.

I still remember some of the boys and girls coming knocking on my door to hang out with me. We played games, video games, went on long walks, and spent quality time together. There were no sexual activities going on with us. We said plenty of jokes as hard cramps in our stomachs took over as we laughed together. Those were the good old times when people actually wanted to have a conversation in person, answer phone calls, return voicemails, and even look at the caller ID.

We had the internet, emails, music playing, going to the pool, playgrounds, and watching movies at each other's homes. There were people coming from the city walking through the wooded areas or finding a ride to Sterling Place. My life had a big transition point of making new friends, adapting to a new environment, but I still really missed living in the city of Coatesville with all of my heart.

I remember the times when my mom would drive the family back to Coatesville and I did not have the same feeling visiting as I did as a resident. This new outlet had me wanting to become a visitor each and every chance I could get. I was happy to go back and get reacquainted with old friends and family members. Then I was left with just a sad feeling once it was time to leave back home to Lancaster.

That, by far, was my biggest struggle-- juggling between two locations knowing full well, I would be resting my head on a pillow in Lancaster. Sometimes my aunts and adult cousins would let me stay the weekend in their homes. I felt somewhat good coming back to visit Ash Park, local churches, the elders in the family, and sometimes go out to eat at my old favorite restaurants.

The time went by quickly during the last two months of my eighth-grade year, and before I knew it, I was getting ready for my 8th grade promotion. I remember this day like it was literally yesterday. It was sunny outside and the other eighth grade students and I were all inside the auditorium. The administrators gave their speeches and music was played very loudly.

After the special awards were handed out to certain students that stood out, our names were announced on an individual level. I saw just about every student being congratulated by their family members and having their pictures taken.

Unfortunately, my mother was not present, and to this day, I am not sure why she was not there. Looking back now, I realize that maybe she was working or taking care of my baby sister. As for my estranged dad, I guess my mom did not tell him or he did not know about me attending Wheatland Middle School. This was a special moment that my parents cannot get back once the time has passed. Educational achievements are just as important as showing up at parent teacher conferences, IEP meetings, PTO meetings, and car-pooling student athletes.

Once certain things are missed out on you just cannot relive those moments again. Sometimes adult parents miss out on the best things that ever happen to them, such as being present in their children's lives all year round. Once those special moments go by, there is no getting them back.

In June 2001, I went to the high school campus for a free physical. There were hundreds of student-athletes present and several doctors and physicians doing all types of tests before signing off at the dotted line for clearance. I was officially a 9th grader at J.P. McCaskey High School, which was a new situation for me.

At this point, I was usually on the campus after school playing sports or being at practices. Signing up for football felt like a new start to my student-athlete journey. I still remember waking up early in the morning for workouts.

First, we went to the weight room to gain strength, power, and put in the gritty work. The coaches and certified weight room trainer were keeping eyes on everybody. We were putting in the work on a consistent basis and always walking away with sore muscles.

Second, we went outside to the football stadium to put in more work. This is when we did the skill drills for each back or line position with the coaches.

Third, were the agility drills that needed to be done correctly or else we started over until it got done right.

Fourth, came the jog up the stadium steps, and doing the 100-meter sprints. The sprints tested every student-athletes will power to see who really wanted to keep moving forward, and still give an honest effort.

As the coaches looked on from the sidelines, they would call out people by their names. There were no favorites to see who crossed the finish line first per group, and hype did not matter at all. The head football coach at that time period was Scott Feldman, along with his great assistants, such as Coach Matt Ortega, Dr. Todd Mealy, Coach Alim Kamara, Coach Pete Susi, Coach George

Savinsky, Coach Chris Booth, Coach Damien Henry, Coach Mark Stauffer, Coach Troy Richardson, and many others.

They did not play any games on the clock. With them, it was always time to take care of business. Under their leadership they molded boys into men, taught life skills during those teachable moments, and helped some of the student-athletes earn full ride athletic scholarships. These coaches earned the trust and respect of the student-athletes, their families, and the Lancaster community.

I remember Coach Damien Henry always encouraged the players to finish the workouts in the weight room, on the track, and during the agility drills. I recall moments when he would call a player out if they were slacking or taking a shortcut. That is because in the game of life there is no room for slacking or somebody else will seize the opportunity for success.

After the summer workouts were completed, it was time for pre-season football camp, and scrimmages. I remember working out with several future Division 1 football athletes such as Perry Patterson, NiQuan Lee, Joey Cross, Danny Melendez, Joel Holler, Tyquan Wright, James Brooks, Charles Brooks, Davon Garcia, Robert Larue, Brandon Way, Zack Wise, and many others. They were leaders that put in the work both on and off the field all year round.

My coaches molded me into having a strong character, mentality, and resiliency. Their words of encouragement spoken during the hot summer days while running the 100-yard dashes certainly did leave a lasting impression with me to this present time period and beyond. While living in poverty I do not remember hearing words of encouragement at home and experiencing a breakthrough.

When I was on the freshman team, what started as a good day of practice turned my life around. I had injured my right wrist before the season officially started. At this point, I was very grateful for Dr. Todd Mealy, a proud alumnus of Millersville University and Penn State Harrisburg Campus.

He always believed in me from the moment we first met each other at J.P. McCaskey High School Campus. He kept encouraging me to show up to football practices and games. Even then, when I fractured my right wrist during football practice, he told everybody to clap it up for me. Once I heard that I felt truly honored & appreciated.

I remember I still needed to support my teammates during the football season. I took on the role of being the water boy for the freshmen boys football team. I did not see myself doing that in the beginning of the season, but I was sacrificing for the team's best interest, showing up to practices even when I was not going to play, and it was worth it.

While being the water boy, I recall the moments like bus rides for away football games and the referees meeting at the 50-yard line with the team captains. During the regular timeouts or injury timeouts, I would sprint to the team huddle with the water bottles to help them stay hydrated. As I started walking back to the sideline to fill up the water bottles, the trainers noticed I was doing a great job even with a hard cast on my right hand.

My teammates, coaches, and peers would sign my red cast with a black sharpie. After wearing the hard cast for several weeks, the doctor said it was time to cut it off. He started testing my wrist out for resistance and strength. I became fully cleared to play football for the last game of the season against Manheim Township high school. I made the most of that opportunity playing several skilled positions and we won the final home game.

I was taught a valuable lesson during my teachable moment. By learning to stay committed to the football team during my injury, I had learned that life does not always work in my favor. Despite that, I still needed to be present even though I did not get much playing time on the football field. Dr. Mealy has taught me to keep growing in education, leadership skills, and the future chapters of my life.

In the winter of 2001, I joined the wrestling team, and several of my teammates were from the freshmen football team. Due to the high school building renovations, our team had to practice and have a few of the wrestling meets at Lincoln Middle School. I remember Sasha Duran from Lincoln middle school. She was very athletic and played several sports as a student-athlete. She tried out for the wrestling team just in case she did not make the Lincoln Middle School girls basketball team. Fortunately, she made both teams.

I'll mention more about Sasha later.

I normally would walk home after practice regardless of the weather or wait until my mom got off work at 11 pm, Sometimes she tried to get me home during her break. I remember a few times during the cold of the winter when Coach Troy, who was coaching me for both football and wrestling during my freshman year, would give me a ride home, just so I did not walk home in the snow or get caught in a heavy rainstorm. It showed he had a heart for those lacking consistent transportation and took time to fill in the void I had in my life.

In the Spring, I joined the freshmen co-ed track team. I ran mid-distance on the track team since other boys were faster than me. Coach Matt Ortega and Coach Kamara helped put each student-athlete in the best position to succeed on the team. Coach Ortega, a proud alumnus of Saint Francis University and Millersville University, was a man of discipline and compassion, was family-oriented, and a great communicator. He encouraged me to get better as I was running on the track and doing football workouts. He always kept the stopwatch in his hand telling me I was making progress.

The practices were conducted both in the football stadium (weather permitting) and inside the high school on rainy days. As a team we ran up and down hills, did "Indian runs", warm-ups, and laps around the track. The bus rides were fun until it was time to take care of business against the home team. Our boys' team was loaded with sprinters, distance runners, throwers, and jumpers. While the girls' team was short on participants, they still remained competitive for their individual events and relays.

I was enjoying my time as a student-athlete until my life changed. While inside the classroom I was told somebody wanted to speak with me. I was not sure who it was until I was taken into a different room with the door closed. A woman introduced herself as a social worker from Children and Youth of Lancaster County.

I guess all those nights of domestic violence and calling the cops finally caught up with my household. Normally, I would go straight to practice or a game after school. Afterwards, I would either have to find a ride home, wait until my mom's break at Conestoga View, or walk home by myself. Once I got home it was me, Ricky, Ronald, and Nancy. The man that was supposed to be there would be caught up with drugs and alcohol binges.

The responsibility would fall on Ricky and Ronald to watch our Nancy until I got home. I was in charge until our mom got home from work. Looking back, having all that responsibility was too much and overwhelming in my life. I was being set up for failure, delays, and more hardships. I was not ready to take care of my younger siblings, and I did not bring them into this world. Being the man of the house is a big task for a young boy.

Once the social worker got involved, all of a sudden, my mom told me to stay home to watch my younger siblings, to cover up everything, and I was forced to sacrifice the next three years of being a varsity student-athlete. She did not want to hire a babysitter or arrange with our neighbors to help in the situation. There was no more time with my teammates, coaches, and creating more to my legacy.

The caseworker must have given my mom an outline to follow, or there would be consequences. After all, it takes a village to raise a child. By me no longer being a student athlete, it caused a delay in me furthering my post-secondary education. I could not get the attention of college scouts to earn an athletic scholarship.

I will admit I was really pissed off at being forced to give up being a student-athlete. That is when I started taking out my frustration on teachers intentionally by causing distractions as the class clown. My teachers and classmates did not deserve it at all. I was a teenager with no way to properly vent, not seeing positive solutions in my household, or any chance at being a student-athlete ever again.

I felt like my world and childhood were stripped away from me. Being a student-athlete was the area of my life where I shined, received praises, compliments, and felt appreciated. I was not getting that from either of my biological parents and my love tank was empty.

A love tank is the part of us that represents our emotional need for love. Once the love tank becomes empty, the worldview becomes narrow and very pessimistic. We have a need for intimacy, affection, words of affirmation, and effective communication. Without a sustainable foundation our love starts to diminish, leading to arguments, estrangement, resentment, and seeking things to fill in the void.

Our natural five love languages are words of affirmation, physical touch, quality time, acts of service, and receiving gifts. Once our love tanks are filled and run over, we function better because we feel appreciated, embraced, and acknowledged in a loving way.

I used to always make the most of each opportunity for gym time to play a game or sport. I usually was the best at running the fastest, being the leader, and my competitive nature came out. This would feed my ego, emotional needs, and self-worth.

Soon after the sport or activity was over, I was right back where I started, and back to my reality. Sure, the gym teachers, learning support teachers, and classmates were very impressed with my speed, agility, athletic skills, and leadership role. I had people's undivided attention on me and it felt good during that time period. I remember one learning support teacher saying that I am blessed with a lot of talent, and I am very special. At the time, I did not understand what she was saying, but I have always remembered that statement.

When I was being a distraction in class, I was held accountable for my actions with warnings and phone calls home. Yet I still got my homework and assignments completed on time for each class I passed. I had a bright future and great opportunity as a student-athlete and a limited time period to leave my mark on the J.P. McCaskey High School Campus, Lancaster City, Lancaster-Lebanon League, District 3, and PIAA. As each year passed, the window was getting closer and closer to being closed.

My relationship changed with my football, wrestling, and track coaches. I was in a no-win situation the last three years of high school. I was still working out on my own time inside of my room. I had all of this energy to channel and no way to use what was building up inside of me.

An important mentor who came into my life around this time was Mr. Clyde E. Brown Jr., son of the late Clyde E. Brown and Elizabeth Emily Easton. Clyde is a proud alumnus of J.P. McCaskey High School and Steven's Tech. He earned a degree in Architecture and helped design many buildings in the Lancaster community.

He grew up on the Southeast side of Lancaster City. He lived his life to be a loving father, caring grandfather, awesome great grandfather, wonderful uncle to several nieces and nephews. Clyde enjoyed working with kids and being heavily involved in the Black History Club. Clyde had a full beard and goatee, often wore glasses, and his sense of humor was very original, creative, and consistent.

I first met Clyde at the Ramada Inn in downtown Lancaster when that was serving as our school building. Mr. Brown caught my attention with his jokes, stories, and discipline. He would make sure to monitor the halls, keeping an eye on everything as he sat at his desk, and wrote people up for detention as needed. Clyde would stop inside the classroom to make sure there was order.

For two years, he would make sure the students enjoyed their lunches and fellowshipped in a respectful manner. He would go on to share stories of being a student-athlete (competing in Varsity football, basketball, and track), family history, childhood memories, and plenty of jokes. When it was time for dismissal, he rang that bell and said “You don’t have to go home but you have to get the h*** out of here.” I used to laugh really hard hearing him say that.

Mr. Clyde would keep a careful eye watching for students doing things they were not supposed to. I once saw two girls smoking cigarettes on school property behind a bus. Little did they know, Clyde was walking with a swagger towards their direction. Once he came up to the girls, he pulled out his pen and notepad to ask “Names, ladies?”. That was one of his famous lines for when he caught female students in trouble. His famous quote to me during lunch period was, (“Ethan is your name. I should tell you to eat some now and eat some later.”)

Later down the road, the McCaskey East building opened back up after the renovations were made and passed the inspections. Mr. Brown was happy to be back on the high school campus, since he literally lived less than two blocks away, putting him within walking distance. The only time he drove his green coupe car to the campus was on a rainy day or when he had to leave early for an appointment or meeting. That was Clyde's way of making his presence known by people.

Eventually, I was placed under the supervision of Clyde because I was the class clown in some of my classes. I had the undivided attention of the classroom, and certain teachers were not cool with it. Honestly, I should have been enrolled into counseling for my underlying pain due to the voids and other things going on in my life. The behavior plans never had positive solutions to heal me and experience the breakthrough of having inner peace that I needed. It is the parents' responsibility to be doing the work with their children. That just was not the case with me and millions of other teenagers around the world.

I was using my sense of humor to feel accepted and wanted. It worked like a charm with a capital C. I would still get my work done and pass the classes. However, I will admit that being in learning support classes did not provide any challenges, just learning the same lesson plans, and curriculum. There is just no fun or excitement in learning the same thing repeatedly.

Under the supervision of Clyde, it was very different being away from certain classrooms. I would be around him in the early mornings to run errands, such as picking up the newspapers from the main office, getting him two cups of coffee with creamers and sugar. Then Clyde had me passing along handwritten notes to other staff (with either tape or a staple on it for privacy reasons).

There were several times I had Mr. Brown laughing so hard he had tears pouring out of his eyes. One time this involved his stomach hurting with cramps causing him to lose control of his bladder. One time at McCaskey East, I was with him during a lunch period, and I saw a girl with really big earrings. I mean bigger than an onion ring. I told Mr. Brown that with the size of those earrings she was wearing she would have a hard time going through an airport's metal detector. His back was against the wall as he laughed non-stop with no regard to the cameras recording our movements.

I remember making some money on the side taking away student's lunch trays for money on the spot. One girl in particular gave me such consistent business that I considered her a faithful clientele. Her name was Jen. She was pregnant as a teenager with a big belly, nice sneakers, and very good-looking outfits. She would make sure her lunch tray was taken away on a priority level.

The old saying goes that when a woman is pregnant, it is advised by doctors she needs to spend the least amount of time on her feet. This can cause a woman's ankles to become swollen, reduce the baby's growth rate, increase preterm delivery, miscarriage, and menstrual disorders. Jen still reminds me to this day what I did for her. Once she had her beautiful baby during the school year, I lost her as a clientele as she left for maternity leave.

Clyde saw how well I did with my side hustle that was under the table, and Uncle Sam could not touch me. The teachers and the support staff noticed there was less drama in the cafeteria and less food messes by me taking up the trays.

Looking back on my time with Mr. Brown, we got along, and related to each other in many ways. I felt like he was playing a pivotal role in my life. Since I did not really see or hear from my estranged father most of the time, just by being around a respected man showed me I did not have to be a distraction in the classroom and show off during gym class. There was life outside of being on the high school campus.

If I wouldn't have been forced to sacrifice my student-athlete journey, I would have been starting varsity football, wrestling, and track. In football, I would have played wideout, corner, and return man. When it comes to wrestling, I do question if I would have stayed committed to that sport. This is because the winter season was the same time indoor track went on. I am sure I would have gotten the athletic director, football, and track coaches input. They would probably have influenced and advised me to focus on just track and football. I believe I would have had a great relationship with several varsity coaches for both football and track. The relationships with my coaches should have been stronger and full of memories to cherish for football, wrestling, and track. If I would have been playing varsity sports instead of watching my siblings, I would have had my national signing day and won gold medals for track and field.

I am sure I would have influenced the crowd to cheer loud and proud. I would have been interviewed by the Lancaster newspaper. Maybe the Late Steve "Bird" Powell would have allowed me to make the varsity and junior varsity basketball teams for the purpose of providing more speed and defense to create fast break points on turnovers. OK, I'm just using my imagination on that personal thought of mine. Maybe I could have been elected to the J.P. McCaskey High School Sports Hall of Fame. Since I did not play any varsity sports during my time at J.P. McCaskey High School, I can still be recognized as a Distinguished Alumni during a varsity football game.

I would have been the fastest sprinter at McCaskey High School, Lancaster -Lebanon League, District Three, and PIAA, holding up the trophies and gold medals with teammates, coaches, and the athletic department. What could have been if the opportunity would have been seized during my teenage years. I am sure my legacy would have been very memorable, and I would have created so many personal memories.

I am not being selfish towards anybody in my life. It is just that when you have athletic ability to impact the high school campus, news reporters, and attract college scouts, you must find your purpose beyond playing varsity sports because there is a great opportunity to earn a full ride athletic or academic scholarship to a college or university.

I did not go to college to further my education right after high school graduation like some students do. Since I did not play any varsity sports, there was no chance to at least earn an athletic scholarship and catch the attention of college scouts. My life had been set up for shortcomings and failure. It led me to following in my older brother's footsteps, working in the food industry at Arby's and Ruby Tuesday's.

I never intended to do the same thing my brother did. It was just that it was my senior year of high school, and I needed to make money to provide for myself as a man. That was the opportunity I chose at the time. Finding jobs was worthwhile to build my resume and keep progressing. The only time I was on a college campus during my years in high school, I was not there for a college tour at all. Instead, I was there to help out inside the dish room at Thaddeus Stevens College of Technology. One benefit of working there was to be given plenty of unlimited food and beverages.

At the time, the quality of food and soft drinks at Steven's Tech was much better quality than the public school. They served nutritious and enjoyable meals. I remember the stir fry was made right in front of me with fresh produce, rice, and meat. The food at a public school was usually in a package reheated inside a commercial size oven. It is normally filled with Genetically Modified Food. It was so unappetizing; I would sell my free lunch for money and save everything up.

I remember getting asked why I stopped playing sports when I had plenty of potential to contribute and make an impact. Nobody but a few people knew how bad my life was behind the scenes. The teachers, coaches, support staff, and administrators knew a social worker was keeping tabs on my family. The social worker would stop by all three schools: elementary, middle, and high school, signing in at the main office for a visitor's pass. Once my younger siblings became teenagers, the social worker finally stopped coming around to visit the schools.

The relief was a new stage. I was no longer being called out of homeroom or class to meet a social worker. Still, sports were an important part of my identity and the way I built relationships. Finding common interests and ground is the game of life. The crowd stays around for the celebrations and holding up the medals and trophies. During the defeats your loved ones and true friends stay around to hold you up.

There was a real financial struggle while I was in my senior year of high school. I was wearing the same clothes since my mom was being negligent with the child support money. She made the situation worse than what it already was. Living in Lancaster Township, there was not any traditional public transportation. This was before a petition and survey was completed, which led to Red Rose transportation providing the bus service as it does today.

Once I graduated from J.P. McCaskey High School, I felt like a free man. No more learning support classes to put me in a box and no more biased education system thinking less of me with my God-given potential and talents.

I had some behavioral problems from my unresolved issues and underlying pain. It did not help to have selective parents, from a single mother to an estranged father that lacked humility and owning their choices. If only they would have aired out their grievances on a priority level, instead of allowing things to burden children.

My first job was at Arby's on Lincoln Highway right across from Dutch Wonderland and right next to the Tanger Outlets. I remember riding the Red Rose shared ride program vehicle. The fare was cheap and affordable. I would get picked up by the vehicle at my home, taken to work, and then picked up for the round trip back home.

The work criteria were doing a little bit of almost everything, such as trash duty, wiping down the windows, cleaning the bathrooms, mopping the floors, making sandwiches, and using the fryer. I was never trained to operate the drive thru or cash register. I was not sure why this was, besides some bogus excuses I heard. You could say this was my humble beginnings of making an honest living, earning $6.50 an hour.

The trips to and from work were very interesting, talking to different drivers, and actually listening to the hit songs played on the radio stations. This goes back to when music was created more organically with real stories, melodies, and relatable things. As soon as you heard the first ten seconds of the intro you knew you were in store for something special. Sometimes I could write poetry both on the way to work and going back home.

Fast forward to working at the Manor Shopping Center. A new chain restaurant was being built called "Ruby Tuesdays." They were well known for grilled burgers, smoked ribs, chicken, pasta dishes, and the salad bar. Once I saw the sign while passing by, I knew it was time to seek a new opportunity and make more money, with the potential of earning $9.50 or more an hour. Adding to the appeal, the location was much closer to my home in Sterling Place. My neighbor helped me fill out the application, and I was called in for an interview.

I was hired on the spot as a dishwasher and prep cook. I was doing almost a little bit of everything except serving alcoholic beverages, cooking on the grill, or using the deep fryer. The manager was Jessy, he was very cool and easygoing with the employees. Jessy would always ask me on the closing shifts "Ethan, can you get me out of here in a reasonable time?

Jessy wanted to get out of there as soon as possible because he wanted to make sure the restaurant was officially closed within two hours after operating hours. Sometimes he would call me on my days off asking me to cover for a dishwasher showing up late or calling off at the last minute. Jessy would make sure I was taken care of with free food, soft beverages, and a ride back home that same night.

One time, Jessy had the playful nerve to make fun of me in front of the cooks in a joking way. It was Easter Sunday on a packed day during the lunch rush orders. Little did he know I had an immediate comeback line to him. I said, "I think I know why you work the closing shift so often, because you have to keep up with paying the child support bunny". He was silent, while the cooks laughed so hard with their hands pressed against their stomachs due to muscle strain. No one ever mentioned that before to Jessy, not ever!

My slick comeback talk did not get me in trouble at all. We just kept on working on Easter Sunday until close.

After continuing to work for two months at Arby's through the probationary period of Ruby Tuesday's, it was time to leave and move on to Ruby Tuesday's full time. So, I gave my written and verbal two weeks notice out of respect to Arby's. While I was working two jobs at the same time, I started feeling the effects in my legs with fatigue from working around the clock.

The money was coming in, but it was not worth feeling overworked. It all slowed down on my last day at Arby's. I only came back two more times to pick up my paycheck. After I handed in my uniform, it was nice leaving on good terms with the extra time on my hands to focus on myself more often. I could finally rest to allow my legs to recover as I only worked at Ruby Tuesday's.

My body felt much better once I started a new routine throughout the week. I stopped using the Red Rose program since there was no set time for me to get off work. Ruby Tuesdays had a better quality of food, drinks, parking space, and experience. While the nice waitresses would do their jobs the right way in good faith, some of the other waitresses were either rude, very unprofessional, or just not cut out to be working as a server. Some of the servers were acting overly dramatic, not following their proper training, and little did they know the managers noticed everything.

They would leave food on the plates and giving me more work to do. I could tell some of them weren't ready to deal with the rude customers and ended up breaking down emotionally to the managers. Jessy would get on them about doing their job right to his dishwasher.

Since he wasn't buying the sob story of someone playing the victim and starting a pity party, Jessy really called them out on the spot by showing them the camera's footage to show their behavior is unacceptable at Ruby Tuesdays, especially, when they were trained to do their jobs the right way. He made sure they understood the training and to treat me with respect. I could tell by Jessy's leadership he had my back every time I came to work.

I was very thankful for making it back home safe and sound from work at night or early morning, even though I had no car or driver's license. Meanwhile, I did what was needed to work, come home, and save my money. Everything was earned, no handouts at all.

Working in the food industry was very time consuming, and a lot of sacrifices had to be made. Now I see why some married couples have such a high divorce rate and families break up. I missed out on family gatherings, events, and much more.

The burning desire I had to make money was the vision. These were the steps I took to get out of poverty, or so I thought. Turns out I was still in the low-income tax bracket. I was still in poverty all that time even with money saved up and my personal needs taken care of.

The thought of furthering my education wasn't even on my mind.

It takes true intentions, ownership, renewing of the mind, and humility to move forward in life. I was making money with so many unresolved burdens. It turns out the real work should have been on myself on an individual level. I realize as an adult that it is no good to make money without the breakthroughs that I needed to deal with my underlying pain. The money I made did not cover the cost of my burdens. Once I gave my life to Jesus Christ in the Spring of 2009, that is when I truly felt free on the inside.

Once a new family moved in next door. His name was Anh Hai. He was from New York and graduated from a high school in North Carolina. Our relationship started out as neighbors and turned into a father-son bond.

We would see each other often, having small conversations. He was usually working to provide and be present for his family. He played some basketball and two-hand touch football with the teenagers in the neighborhood of Sterling Place. After I was dropped off by the school bus, I would start cooking food, and it caught Anh Hai's attention. He was wondering what I was making and wanted to try some. Next thing I knew, we were having lunch and dinner together on the regular.

He helped me open my first bank account for both checking and savings. One time my tire had a nail, and Anh Hai told me I needed to go straight to the Tire Place. Luckily, I was right down the street, and my tire was patched up in no time. Soon, I was back on the road driving again. We attended a Philadelphia 76ers basketball game together. I can say it was a father-son moment taking a selfie together in the arena.

We started playing each other in video games like Madden NFL Football and ESPN NFL 2K5. I remember we scored four touchdowns in a span of less than two minutes against each other. That competitive nature to channel my energy into video games led me to be a pro video gamer later on in the adult years of my life.

What ultimately led me to my decision to go pro was an evening I spent at a girl's home getting my hair braided. I remember watching TV as she was parting my hair into sections. The MTV Channel came on as though I had found my calling to be a pro video gamer. I remember the show was about pro video gamers making a living by playing.

I am talking about earning straight cash and checks but sometimes under the table income. Once I saw people playing NFL Madden Football, I was sold and ready to get started right away. It was time for me to go Pro and make money through victories.

I practiced the game for countless hours, studying, researching, and applying new user game features for a complete competitive advantage. My user skills transitioned from average to above average and to elite. My favorite team to play with was the Philadelphia Eagles with the West coast Offense and top ranked defense. Donovan McNabb was the dual-threat quarterback leading the offense and the Brian Dawkins was leading the hard-hitting defense.

I could beat anybody for money and did not mind playing for double or nothing during the good old days of riding the train to Philadelphia, Harrisburg, Coatesville, and back to Lancaster. I was use to beating people with the twenty-one-rule meaning once a player is winning by twenty-one points, the other player has one last chance to score on the kickoff or the other player wins.

One time, while working at Ruby Tuesdays, a co-worker covered for me on a closing shift. I ended up taking the Amtrak Train to Philadelphia at 69th St. Station. I took the Septa bus to King of Prussia Mall to compete in the Madden Tournament.

Sure, I took a few losses along the way to reflect on the game and get better. I remember dreaming of playing on the ESPN Madden Bus Show, sponsored by Best Buy & EA Sports. The top pro video gamers in the USA were competing in tournaments. I dreamed of reaching higher heights of glory and fame with being a pro video gamer.

The final two players left standing from the Madden bus tour would be competing for $100,000.00 in the middle of Time Square, New York. My dream came to an abrupt halt once the economy crashed in 2008. The game show was canceled, the cash prizes for the tournaments was reduced to much lower amounts.

It was fun while it lasted for me being a pro video gamer. I am still very good at playing NFL Madden to this day, but I rarely play the game system now, as I put more focus on my life and personal development. I ended up moving on to the poetry and spoken word scene.

Looking back on my time with Anh Hai, we both played a key role in each other's lives. He was the adult man while I was the teenager going through difficult phases in my life. I needed a relationship like that, given everything that took place during that time period. I did not get caught up in the street life, drugs, drinking excessive alcoholic beverages, or a teen pregnancy, but I also missed out on being a student-athlete, prom, homecoming, dances, and senior night events.

I was not distracted even though I had deep voids in my life. I was simply keeping my mind active on other things to stay on the right path. I certainly did not want to be arrested for anything stupid or life changing. While my younger siblings were under my guidance, I was not fit to be the man of the house. I was only a teenager going through a tough situation. I cannot turn back the hands of time or change the decisions that were made during that time period.

Chapter 4. Finding God

Growing up, I remember attending church services and being in the youth group. Looking back, I realize a few things that went through my mind. Since Easter Sunday is supposed to be about Jesus Christ dying on the cross for our sins. I observed people being involved with Easter egg hunts, coloring eggs, and making a big deal about a commercial idol- the Easter Bunny. Some things just did not add up.

My grandmother Alberta and I would attend church, pay tithes, and offerings. Most churches are non-profit organizations either non-domination or domination for charity or tax write offs. My grandmother would come home ready to make Sunday dinner, a family tradition. I feel like more work on a relationship with God is done away from church or places of worship.

In 2007, I was invited to bible study, and I was a little hesitant, but I accepted the invite. The setting was more personal, with no choir, no music band, no pastor preaching at the pulpit, or extra activities. The circle we made was round, and conversations of dialogue started answering my questions about life.

I made the big choice to get saved and give my life to God. The excitement was building up as people would say "You are making the best choice of your life". There were people behind the scenes willing to help with the ceremony, food, and drinks. I felt a sense of humility when I admitted that I am a sinner in front of everybody. I normally did not do public speaking at all. I would stay away from the spotlight most of the time. This time it was a big step towards growing as a man.

As I got ready to go through with the baptism into the pool of water, I saw the crowd grow large with the praise and worship singing. As Steve King spoke a statement about the Father, Son, and Holy Ghost, I felt a new life start within me. I heard the cheers, applause, and statements of people being proud of me. On May 5th, 2009, I entered a new chapter, and the wedlock curse was broken away from me.

Now I could start a new, productive behavior pattern, continuing to break the chains of other negative behavior. Once I started confronting what needed to be addressed and reading people's body language better, I began a period of growth.

Giving your life to Christ does come at a cost. No credit card, invoice, or direct deposit can cover this bill. I started growing apart from some people, distancing myself from others. I changed my appearance, looking at life differently, and, of course, finding my true purpose on Earth.

I felt good getting baptized, receiving my plaque, and having my picture taken several times. It was clear to me that a brand-new start was needed in 2009. I soon realized there was more work to be done in my life from the inside and out. One day I ran into a man named Billy with a successful business, big family, and big farmland. He offered to sponsor me for a Door of Hope conference at Lancaster Bible College. I was not even sure what Billy was talking about when the offer was made.

Then suddenly another man named Timmy offered to give me rides to the Conference. I said yes as it seemed like it was worth looking into. I soon realized the Door of Hope is a Discipleship Ministry changing lives on an "inside job" level.

They had several guest speakers covering a wide variety of topics such as spirit, soul, and body. They soon moved on from the surface, going much deeper into people's hearts to address negative life experiences. During the five-day conference, I started to experience freedom on a higher level. I had some unresolved deep-rooted issues that had turned into underlying pain and repressed memories.

As a child and teenager, I had unknowingly put off the things that needed to be addressed. I did not know I was suppressing those issues, and I wasn't given the closure I needed to move forward. I had not been given the tools, knowledge, or wisdom on how to overcome a troubled past.

Door of Hope provided me with the opportunity to remove the excess baggage that I was carrying in my life. I left it all at the cross and did not look back. The leaders prayed over me about things I did not truly know about, going all the way back to my ancestors.

Once I started confronting these things, a big weight had been lifted off me. On the last day of the conference, I remember leaving with more strength, knowledge, and confidence than I had when I arrived.

Finding God is necessary to find inner peace towards living a life that in certain moments seeks to glorify the creator of all things. The following steps can be found in the bible to learn a wealth of knowledge from other people's personal lessons, passions, and life choices.

Following or seeking the will of God. Our plan is not always better than God's own plan for our lives. He sees things or situations so far ahead to know the beginning, middle, and the end. To trust his will takes vulnerability on a physical, emotional, spiritual level. That takes faith to put down the defense mechanism. The time invested for a person to be that vulnerable on a social, cognitive, and environmental level shows their willingness to transform from being a victim into a victor.

Once you discover you are living a purpose driven life, applying God's principles, and overcoming personal challenges, always make time for prayer, while seeking clear direction, clarity, understanding, and guidance. The journey to attain peace and gain a sense of faith is through prayer. Prayer is always available for people to articulate a situation, trauma, drama, or deep underlying pain, or unresolved issues. Once a person can start seeking answers to give closure, they may begin to live by faith and not by sight.

I have seen church meetings, guest speakers, revivals, special conferences, and people either seeking salvation or praying. One time while visiting a mission in Brooklyn, I overheard a stranger confessed to murdering somebody with a gun, yet he was filled with guilt and shame for his wrongful actions.

I was confused as to why the stranger did not just turn themselves to the police, allow justice to be served, give victims loved one's closure, and pay his debt to society. I guess in the stranger's situation he was seeking relief instead of doing the right thing for the greater good.

In between the hyphen of a headstone is your legacy, memories, stories, journey's, hardships, chapters you have entered and finished. I could have thrown the white towel into the boxing ring, but I did not. Giving up too soon leaves questions. What if you finished what you could have committed to?

What if you stayed the course? There is a difference between suffering and being stressed out. Suffering is enduring pain, distress, or severe hardships. Some stress levels can also be feeling overwhelmed, overburdened, unable to cope with mental or emotional, acute, episodic, acute, and chronic stresses.

I went through a very traumatic experience. By the grace of God, I was able to function at my lowest point in life.

Chapter 5.

Car Accident and Recovery Pt.1 – "The Day my Life Changed Forever"

I remember seeing Jordan Steffy on WGAL's Football Friday, Lancaster Newspaper, and various social media outlets. Jordan graduated from Maryland University on a full ride Athletic scholarship and Columbia University with an MBA. One Saturday evening, I decided to attend a Saturday evening church service at In the Light Ministries. I sat down and a few moments later, Jordan sat next to me, and I had to ask him "Are you Jordan Steffy?". He said yes and shook my hand. I was really shocked he was even near me, he looked very different in person as I usually saw him on television. I suppose the timing was right with meeting the right person.

After the service was over, we engaged in a great conversation, decided to connect on social media, and exchange cell phone numbers. Jordan was in his mid-20's then, just a couple years older than me, but he had already accomplished so much as varsity student-athlete, collegiate student-athlete, and started a non-profit foundation.

After that evening, we kept running into each other by coincidence in Lancaster City. We both just kept picking up right where we left off. Then he introduced me to his family and girlfriend, now wife and mother of his kids, Mrs. Kiandra Bair-Steffy. I went to the same high school as Kiandra, J.P. McCaskey High School. At the time, his non-profit was called Children Deserve a Chance Foundation. It has since been renamed Attollo.

Jordan was planning an event at the Lancaster Convention Center in downtown Lancaster. I just so happened to have a poem about

Michael Vick's situation and the guest speaker was Michael Vick. My poem was presented in front of a crowd of over 4,000 people. This event was for the Michael Vick's redemption after serving his debt to society. The experience was truly amazing to shake his hand, take pictures with him, have lunch, and give him a card.

You never know where your journey of faith is going to lead you.

I can point to the day I was involved in a near fatal car accident on Saturday, March 19, 2011. This was the exact moment my life was forever changed. As I remember waking up on a hospital bed, I knew something was not right. Nobody was telling me anything, since they were fearing my blood pressure would get too high.

May you imagine the firefighters cutting the car in half with the jaws of life while being in the midst of trying to not harm anyone with debris?

May you imagine the police directing traffic and using the yellow tape to keep citizens away from hazards such as, downed power lines, gas leaks, fire scenes, and many other dangerous obstacles?

May you imagine the paramedics taking your pulse to find out if you heart is pumping enough blood, to help find the cause of symptoms such as, an irregular or rapid heartbeat, dizziness, fainting, chest pain, or shortness of breath?

May you imagine people calling 9-1-1 seeking immediate help? May you imagine how hard it will be seeing two people die on sudden impact of the fatal car accident, while two other people are alive, and yet another person's life hangs in the balance of a mathematical equation?

May you imagine traffic being backed up for several miles, while the other people's errands and priorities are put on hold?

I am just trying to help you, the reader, visualize the traumatic effects of my near-death experience. The statement read above is only me using my imagination of what possibly took place during a certain time period. As I have said countless times before, I have never seen a head on collision, between an 18-wheeler and a car take place, even though I was there to experience everything firsthand. Since time only moves forward in life, those critical seconds, minutes, and countless hours were ticking away, while my life hung in great despair: death vs life.

The near fatal car accident scene was like a dramatic movie with a life or death situation. The news reporters traveled from far distances trying to be the first to capture the accident and give a breaking news report. I understand they have a job to do with the media and providing footage on a last-minute notice. They must have felt sad to report a couple of people passed away, two were injured, and one was in critical condition. That person in critical condition was me facing a ninety-nine percent chance of death vs one percent chance of life.

Saturday, March 19th, 2011, was the day my life changed forever. I was at Meadia Heights Golf Course with Jordan Steffy, his family members, donors, board members, and several guests. We were trying to sell Deuce watches to raise money for the Children Deserve a Chance foundation. Overall, we surpassed our fundraising goal, and it felt great.

I left the event with my Aunt Tancy and her fiancé. We went to pick up both of my cousins and then headed home. Little did I know that my life was about to change forever. I had no idea this was about to happen on a sunny Saturday afternoon.

As I was riding inside a four-door sedan on Route 30, I remember watching clothing stores, fast food restaurants, the American Music Theater, Ruby Tuesdays, the Nike outlet, and many more establishments go by. The last thing I remember seeing was the Hess gas station.

Around 3:30 pm in front of 3437 Lincoln Highway East, about one-fourth a mile west of Vintage Road, the state police, fire department, and ambulance arrived at the scene of the car accident of an 18-wheeler tractor-trailer and a Jeep.

As I look back on my Facebook timeline from March 2011, I see all the comments of people saying their prayers for me and my family. I get this warm feeling in my stomach that people actually cared about me even in the midst of uncertainty with my health.

On March 24th, 2011 Jordan Steffy left a message on my wall stating this quote, "Ethan Update: Today was by far Ethan's best day! He is talking and in a lot less pain. He still has a long road to being fully recovered and will most likely have to have a final surgery on his collar bone, but he is in stable condition and even recited a poem this evening!!! Good night, all." As I read that statement updating people on my health, I feel really touched by seeing those words as they resonate in my heart. He was definitely right about a long road to recovery.

Next thing I knew, I woke up almost a week or two later in the ICU not knowing why I was even there. I just noticed that I was lying down in a hospital bed with tubes in my chest, IVs in my veins, and nobody was telling me anything. Two days passed, and finally somebody told me that I had been involved in a near fatal car accident, and I should have died.

I heard what was said, but it did not truly resonate with me as a whole. I was on a long list full of prescription medicines and my inner feelings were still numb to me. My body was literally desensitized my nerve endings from the medicines.

Once the near fatal car accident happened, everything was taken away except for my life. As I rested on an anticipated death bed at Lancaster General Hospital, it affected all areas of my life. There was little hope, barely even a prayer. My heart suddenly stopped, leading to calls to the coroner and the forensic team. But as my life seemed to be coming to an end, I knew and believed there was more to life than what I had imagined and was living.

Can you imagine going from feeling your body's five senses to only feeling like something is not right?

I do not remember the first visitors to see me. I was legally high on the medicine to cope with serious trauma, injuries, and often put to sleep. The effects of the prescription medicine were helping me to recover from the pain and start the long road to being functional again. People must have been shocked to get the phone call that I was fighting for my life. The headlines were on social media, television stations, radio stations, and in the Lancaster Newspaper.

I can only imagine the news coverage was receiving a lot of viewers. The churches were taking prayer requests on a priority level for me and other people involved.

When I overcame the odds of death from a near fatal car accident, many people's prayers were answered. Without God answering those prayers, I would not even be here anymore. The funeral arrangements and burial never did happen. The announcement of my death was never made or published in the newspaper, news reporters, or social media. People never did say their final farewells, pay their respects, or see me one last time. My testimony is filled with grace, mercy, favor, and a full recovery.

Inside the Lancaster General Hospital, I was told I am a Walking Living Miracle. I did not fully understand what that meant. I just knew I had survived a serious car accident and my life was forever changed.

God chose to prevent my funeral arrangements, an obituary, a graveside burial, and people from mourning, and grieving. It was not my time to leave this earth and die young. I can only imagine my funeral being packed reaching beyond maximum fire code capacity. I am sure people would have told funny stories, memories, and shared special moments.

As for now, my gravestone has not been created yet. Instead, I am able to create positive memories and connect with people every day. Hopefully my funeral can wait until I live a full life and create a bigger legacy.

Keep in mind I was fully awake before the near fatal car accident took place. I may have blacked out from such blunt force trauma. This is a serious injury caused by forceful impact to the body from the severe impact resulting from the head on collision. I do not remember anything that took place from the start, middle, or ending of that accident. If I did remember anything, I could have suffered from serious post-traumatic stress. I still have no symptoms or diagnoses of any PTSD.

How amazing it is to hear firsthand from me. The doctors conducted several tests on me and they all came back negative for PTSD. They were truly shocked by the results.

A concussion can do damage to the brain, and the recovery process varies on a case-by-case level. I can say my recovery took some time while being on a feeding tube, severely underweight, and on prescription medicine.

There was a long journey ahead of me while my life was on a downward turn. The nurses coming into my room gave me around the clock care while I stayed put inside the hospital bed with an IV's inside of my veins and a monitor constantly beeping. The bed sheets, linens, pillowcases, and food trays were changed daily.

The chaplain visited me to ask me questions, said a prayer, and came back a few more times. I had visitors each day coming to Lancaster General Hospital. My doctor's orders were very strict. I was told I needed to rehab to regain my strength, vocal motor skills, and generally get my life back in order.

During the speech therapy sessions, I had to start all over again with practicing my vocals and sounding out words. That was the effect of a serious concussion and having the breathing tube down my throat for so long. The serious head injury required an MRI, and my brain was still healing with spots of blood. My strength was very weak from losing so much blood and weight.

I was experiencing a very challenging recovery process, and that was my reality. My faith was tested in more ways than you could ever imagine. Reading the bible helped me take my mind off my personal struggles. I could have given up at any moment, but I never did.

I enjoyed my time at Lancaster Rehabilitation. This time I had a whole room to myself, and visitors still came by to see me. I remember that I enjoyed watching the NCAA March Madness Basketball Tournament that year in the room. I became used to getting visitors who were always on their best behavior, with no drama, and nobody asking me for money or favors. They were just people taking time out of their lives to see me as I was making progress.

The visitors offered me their sincere undivided attention for my best interest and wellbeing. There were plenty of prayer requests made on my behalf. I remember a nurse named Eli telling me not to touch the catheter to help me pee. I always appreciated visitors sacrificing their time and putting their life on hold to show they cared about a life that was not theirs.

During this time, I was relearning everything: walking, talking, grabbing things, and doing small muscle building activities. My schedule was on track to make progress and stay committed. Reading the Lancaster newspaper felt very refreshing to see what was going on in the world since my life was put on hold for recovery.

One day, I was still not anywhere near 100% with my health when I woke up inside of my room at the rehab. I noticed there was peace and a silent time period for privacy. One of the nurses allowed me to use her Apple iPhone to check on my social media.

I had seen several unread messages inside my inbox and countless social media posts about the car accident. I felt overwhelmed when telling people the whole truth about why I replied back so late. They were in a state of shock after realizing my life almost ended and I was still alive in recovery mode.

Unfortunately, I had to go through some more adversity. One day while eating lunch, I started to choke on a banana I was eating. One of the nurses saw my struggle and quickly told her supervisor. Once again, I ended up back at the Lancaster General Hospital, this time for a feeding test. I had to consume a chalky liquid for the doctors to see what was wrong with my eating skills. I completed the testing and was about to leave when the paramedic's cell phone rang, and we had to immediately head right back to the hospital, this time for emergency feeding tube surgery.

Can you imagine having a normal stomach one day, then a feeding tube the next, helping you to barely stay alive?

I remember seeing mentor Jordan Steffy, his friend, John Carpenter, and a few other people around me. I was not sure what was going on besides being told "You'll be alright, Ethan." Post-surgery, I was told that I would not be allowed to eat any food or drink any liquids. I was shocked at this news, but the doctor said that I would get pneumonia if I did not comply with the orders.

Pneumonia is when inflammation occurs inside the air sacs in your lungs that may become filled with fluid or pus. The infection can be very life threatening to anyone. Stage one is congestion as the lungs become very heavy and congested due to the infection. Stage two is when red blood cells and immune cells enter the fluid filled lungs to fight off the infection. Stage three is when gray hepatization occurs in the lungs and strong symptoms still persist.

I definitely did not want to suffer anymore to make my health much worse than how it was at the time. It took discipline to follow the doctors' orders and get used to not consuming any food or liquids. I had to sleep with a towel underneath my mouth since it was so watery. That is how I was sleeping most nights on my bed.

My left collar bone fracture never healed properly, causing me to not have surgery due to my right vocal cord being paralyzed at that time. My left collar bone looks very different from my other non-fractured collar bone. I had to sleep on either my back or right side, and my left arm was inside a sling for several months.

I remember asking for a cup of water from the nurse. She had a popsicle stick with a sponge on the tip and dripped it inside the water. I was told to raise my mouth as only one tiny drop of water was felt on my tongue. I wondered what was going on and felt as though I was being teased because I was still very thirsty.

I realized being on a feeding tube was helping me stay alive for the better or worse. But the journey kept me wondering if I would ever consume beverages and food ever again. The thought was on my mind a lot as time passed by. Eventually, I began walk more often inside the rehab center with a feeding tube still attached to my stomach.

Jordan Steffy and his family would visit me at Lancaster General Hospital, Lancaster Rehab, and at my home. They were faithful in being by my side as the recovery process was very long and enduring for several months.

I was on a feeding tube for five months. It could have been 7 months or longer if I had not been persistent with getting a second opinion from the Ear, Nose, & Throat Doctor. To pass the time, I began reading the Bible every day to keep my mind on something else besides eating. My body was very weak because I had lost over 60 pounds, and I became sensitive to light from the concussion. I missed out on attending student's 5th and 8th grade promotions at the local schools, high school graduation ceremonies, birthday parties, and having a sense of independence.

My life had all of this down time while I was on the feeding tube. The average person's downtime is devoted to finishing their bucket list and going on vacation. My downtime consisted of resting, rehab, and staying in prayer. The only times I left the home were with somebody else for my doctor's appointments, church, and sometimes going to a park.

Outside of that, I was depending on passing a feeding test to start eating again. Without normal food I was living each passing day as though the adversity was something I would not be overcoming. I had to keep my mind busy on something else.

Prior to the accident, I was supposed to enroll at Harrisburg Area Community College, go for my driving test, and start a new job. Once again, I was reminded about the effects of the accident that took those opportunities away. However, I was still grateful for the people who continued to take time out of their lives to come visit me at home, the hospital, and in rehab.

Going through speech therapy and physical therapy was a humbling experience at Lancaster Rehab. I was sounding out words, vowels, and finally speaking complete sentences. The journey to regain my high vocabulary IQ was a very challenging task in itself. I realized the road to a full recovery was very far away.

Doing the neck, arm, and leg workouts kept me moving in the right direction. The progress came over time as I made a consistent effort. Relearning how to walk again without the use of a wheel chair took a big push. The doctors wanted me out of the wheelchair and walking several times around the building or they would have to start using blood thinners to prevent a blood clot. I did not get too comfortable depending on a wheelchair. Being underweight and on a feeding tube challenged every fiber I had left within me. The mental and physical elements of my recovery were a mighty task to overcome.

I can recall during football practice my athletic coaches saying to give it everything you have left during the practices and games or wrestling matches. I remember a moment in a movie called "Facing the Giants," when two players were doing the death crawl during a football drill with one teammate on the top using their legs, while the other teammate was on his back.

The coach said strong words of encouragement to keep the player motivated to use their legs to power them. You give your very best without rest until there is nothing left. There is always more left in the love tank even when it hurts the most. You have to keep going and not quit on yourself. Find it within your heart of hearts to finish what you started. You cannot go about your life looking and feeling defeated. The game of life has a time limit and an expiration date. I just couldn't give up on myself, the people that were praying for me, the people that believed in me, and

In the summer of 2011, the doctor's switched my diet from one liquid to a completely different liquid that contained dairy, a substance I am allergic to. The doctor's told me it would help me gain more calories. But it all backfired as I was starting to feel worse than before. I was throwing up nonstop and started feeling weaker until I knew it was time to call the ambulance for immediate help.

It was a very humbling experience to call for help on an emergency level. The paramedics arrived knocking on the front door, and

Ricky had opened up the door for them. I was placed on a stretcher and put inside the ambulance.

Once I arrived inside the emergency room, they started asking questions about what was wrong with me and more details. After I was released from Lancaster General Hospital, I was back home feeling no better than before. One time my mom called for an emergency doctor's appointment with my primary care physician. He had noticed I was not looking right at all, as I was hunched over barely able to sit up straight, and my health did not appear to be good.

The doctor said I needed to go back to the Lancaster General Hospital ICU right away. Once my mom drove me back to the hospital, the nurses put me back on the previous liquid, and I started feeling better within a few days. Again, I had visitors come see me as I was back inside a hospital bed. Once the doctors finally discharged me, I was back home again.

That experience was very exhausting mentally, physically, and emotionally. I do not wish that on anybody at all. I was on modern medicine to cope with my serious injuries. The doctors prescribed it to me and the list was very long, like a child's Christmas list.

Modern medicine was designed to help a person cope with pain, mental health illness, and other things. In some cases, with prescription medicine, the medicine can turn into a serious addiction if the person does not work on healing their underlying pain.

In my situation, I was prescribed a lot of medicines for my serious injuries and on-going pain. I would take the medicine for several months as my situation was further delayed due to being underweight and not being able to consume food or liquids. Even when I was in the hospital and rehab, I was still fighting for my life. I had to make sure the feeding tube was clean and did not get clogged.

Since I was having all this down time, it became too much on my hands as all I could do was stay at home. I would reflect on how my life was forever changed with each passing day and night. There was no telling when my situation would become better.

The opioid crisis is a very serious situation going on in the world. I have come to realize that people are trying to play doctor with their deep underlying pain that is left unresolved. Not everyone gets to reclaim their life and live in sobriety. I did not become a statistic of criminal arrest, court ordered rehab, a drug addict, or an overdose needing a dose of Narcan (aka Naloxone) to save my life.

I am very thankful for not having an addiction to any of the prescription medicines. As I was being weaned off everything step by step, there were less medicines being prescribed to me, and I started feeling like myself again. But then, reality hit me: I was starting to realize I missed out on so much, and this time there was no medicine to use when trying to cope with all this emotional pain.

I was in a place where my emotions started coming back to me, and there was no hiding from them. I realized there were a couple of people who passed away from the car accident. I was not able to pay my respects at the funeral or burial.

There are plenty of resources made available to cope with, function, and experience breakthroughs. The blueprint requires a committed work ethic all year round. You have to do the work behind closed doors and when nobody's looking. That is what I did after my discharges from Lancaster General Hospital and Lancaster Rehab.

On a side note, April 20th, 2011, I was discharged to go home from the hospital. On April 28th, 2011 a special anointing was done at my home for healing both parts of my throat. I requested this because my life on the long road to recovery was very rocky. This experience was like no other, having my health hanging by a thread. As for my birthday on May 23rd, I could not even celebrate, eat, or drink. There were plenty of comments on my Facebook profile wishing me Happy Birthday. August 20th, 2011, the doctors said I would not be having surgery on my collar bone since it healed on its own from the fracture I really wanted my body to be fully healed.

For me, being underweight and on a feeding tube was a daunting way to live. I was often posting poetry on Facebook to stay positive at my lowest point.

On August 4th, 2011, I started eating and drinking again. I was due for another feeding test to see if I could begin eating normally again. I was hoping and praying for the best results. After completing the feeding test, I passed and was allowed to start eating soft foods again. About one month later a doctor removed the feeding tube, and although it was a very painful experience, I was excited and ready to get my life back on track.

Over time, I became more able to tolerate pain and channel my emotions by using more common sense, knowledge, wisdom, and favor. I am not sure how to describe the feeling facing life's challenges with positive solutions and continue to go on living. It did not come through military training, somebody yelling orders, or corporal punishment.

Overall, I did survive a near fatal car accident with an 18-wheeler and was supposed to die within minutes of internal bleeding. It was God who allowed the 1% alive to defeat the 99% of death. God sure does know how to redo math problems regardless of the greatest common fraction. God is the creator of both the numerator and denominator. God has a way of doing the unthinkable for those he truly gave purpose for their life on earth. He makes sure the faith and works are in unison together.

Chapter 6. Homeless

Unfortunately, my next tribulation was right around the corner. Shortly after the time I left the hospital, I received a summons to magisterial court. I did not understand why this was happening to me, when I knew I did not do anything wrong or commit a crime. I was shocked, in disbelief and confused. When I showed up to court I was told that I owed $2000.00 in back rent.

Luckily, the plaintiffs did not file the right paperwork to proceed with the civil claim for back rent, so the judge dismissed the case. I looked at Dorsey wondering why I was even here, and as always, she just gave me the complete run around. That was a definite red flag.

After this mishap, I started picking up on things about Dorsey's behavior pattern. I found out that she was giving away all of her working wages to a con man over the internet. He gave her false promises of love and always told her that he could not wait to see her in person. This of course was a lie and never happened. For anybody to do that it must mean some serious mental health issues are going on. A grown man is called to provide, protect, and profess his life for others. This con man did not have any of those qualities.

I eventually confronted Dorsey about this situation, and she just waved me off. Then, I got summoned to court once again for the second time in a row. This time the Plaintiffs had the right paperwork and won a judgment for back rent. I looked at my mom with displeasure, anger, and wondered how she could do this to our family. My two irresponsible adult brothers did not even bother showing up to court. There was another summon to court for a third time in a row, this time for failing to pay the judgment in which the judge ruled in the Plaintiffs favor again.

By the time I got summoned to court for a 4th time in a row, I knew at this point I had nothing to lose by testifying against Dorsey and defending myself as a grown man. At the time, I had no idea what squatter rights were, but that was what I was left with. My heart had grown very heavy for knowing the truth about her actions and for being associated with someone that was making my life and livelihood worse.

I was given a ride to the magistral court. As I was waiting inside the lobby to be called in, the plaintiffs showed up, then shortly after Dorsey showed up. She was very surprised to see me there. The bailiffs called everyone inside the courtroom. The judge was looking displeased to find the same case for the fourth time. As the plaintiffs said the judgment was not paid in full, and they were ready to file for eviction and possession.

The judge said does anyone on the defense have anything to say. I raised my hand telling the judge "I want to speak your honor."

Once I took the stand and said the oath, with one hand up and the other hand on the Bible, I testified against Dorsey. I told the judge about my entire health situation and how Dorsey was giving away her working wages to a con man over the internet. The plaintiffs were shocked at hearing the news, and the expression on their faces was priceless. I pretty much let the cat out of the bag and set it free. The judge was blown away by my testimony and believed me.

Dorsey sat on the defendant's side of the courtroom and called me a liar - pleading with the judge to not believe me. The court room went silent for almost ten seconds as I changed the case moving forward. Dorsey is an adult and was making adult choices by breaking the lease agreement. When a tenant fails to pay the rent, it is considered a breach of contract. That is when the legal system takes over by going through the eviction process.

The judge said, "The next time I see you in my courtroom there will be an eviction." The whole court room went silent. In the end, I felt relieved with a clear conscience. My heart was no longer heavy. I knew my relationship with Dorsey was completely damaged and would never again be the same.

After leaving the courtroom on the day that I testified against Dorsey, there was a sudden change in my life. I knew my life was entering a new phase. After attending Bible study, I went back home, and there she was yelling curse words telling me "I want you out." Once I entered my room some of my personal belongings were already packed up by her. There was no more fight left in me after going through so much drama and chaos with her. I could have called the cops on her for harassment and invasion of privacy but the energy I had left needed to be used in other areas of my life.

I never thought I would be leaving my mom's home on those harsh terms. Again, I just did not see myself living there anymore, even prior to me testify against her in the courtroom. The following day I felt like it was best to distance myself from my mom even more. The relationship reached a bitter end and boiling point of no return.

Now I know you are wondering how I could go from surviving a near fatal car accident to passing the feeding tests to consume food and beverages again to facing eviction to being homeless. Honestly Dorsey was setting me up for failure during the worst times of my health. I have learned that not everybody that is close to you has your best interest at heart. Usually, it is the people that are the closest to you that either protect or hurt you the most.

The day I moved out created a new reality for me, as I moved into my friend's home, and started a new life of my own. A couple of trucks arrived at Dorsey's home, and I stepped outside while the guy had a brief talk with my mom. Afterwards, we started loading up the trucks with my personal belongings. I said my final goodbye to my room, which now belonged to Ricky.

I was off to a brand-new start under these hardships, and it was time for me to fend myself as an adult. I never enrolled in or stayed at the Water Street mission or any shelter (probably because I was too handsome looking to be in there). All jokes aside, I already had a place to stay.

Honestly, I just did not see myself going that low in my life to hit a new rock bottom. The homelessness did not break me at all. Just think about the movie "The Pursuit of Happiness." The situation in that movie was the blueprint on how to keep moving forward in my life and stand on your own two feet. I started looking at my life with a different perspective. I did not go looking for an apartment, since I had 3 judgments against me, and that's a major red flag with the landlord associations, property managers, and private landlords.

Do you know how it feels to fill out a change of address form on your own? Have you ever testified against any of your parents, and family members? Can you relate to being kicked out of your parents home?

I did not speak or see my mom for several months. She had already told her story to family members and her friends to portray herself as the victim. There were many things said about me from Dorsey that I heard from other people. But I told the whole truth about what really happened.

Being homeless was part of the journey towards getting my life back together; it was not going to be the story for the rest of my life. I never slept in abandoned buildings, on the streets, parks, or pavilions. Church leaders would suggest I go to the Water Street Mission for help and get back on my feet. I was not really interested in that choice and kept living my life.

My confrontation with my mom was a "no turning back" moment leading up to everything changing in my life during that time period. It was at this time that I made a conscious effort to focus on my personal growth, get my life back on track, and overcome all of my prior adversities. I did not want to make any excuses as to why I could not achieve my goals. For a better quality of life, I needed to make something of myself. Even though I was homeless, I felt more at peace being away from my mom, than being around her.

Moving forward, I would meet a man named Tyler while attending a middle school basketball game. I did not know at the time he would turn out to be a positive influence in my life. After the game was over, I went to the bathroom and ran into Tyler who had been in one of the stalls. We had talked really briefly, then he suggested we exchange contact information to stay in contact.

He texted me that we needed to meet at a food place. I showed up at a McDonald's and received a text saying he was going to be late. I had left McDonald's and ended up coming back later on that day. We regrouped almost two hours later for the meeting. Once he finally arrived inside the parking lot, he apologized for being really tardy.

We started talking about life, sports, music, and suddenly he opened up about his past mistakes. I realized he was giving his testimony and pouring out his heart. I shared some information about what I had been through and how I was living my life.

He was totally surprised and shocked. He did not see me as a man recovering from a near fatal car accident and living in-between homes. I noticed he held a strong faith in God to restore the broken foundation of anybody.

The day of my birthday, I attended an alumni meeting at J.P. McCaskey High School. We were going over the agenda, upcoming events, and fundraising ideas. After the meeting was over, I noticed there was some rain outside, and I was offered a ride by one of the men that had attended the meeting.

He dropped me off at College Avenue to attend a Poetry Paths event at Franklin and Marshall College. I enjoyed hearing those kids speak poetry in their own words. They would go on to describe certain environments in the City of Lancaster. The way those statements sounded were very eye opening and captured the listening ears of the audience. I saw myself in them for the love of poetry.

After the event was over, I noticed the rain had stopped, and I started walking to the Lancaster Marriott Hotel. I was waiting in the valet area for Tyler to pick me up. Once he arrived, I hopped inside his car. We fulfilled our plan to have dinner at Apple Bee's.

He treated me to dinner for my birthday to celebrate my life. We started talking about how I was going to move forward in my life. I remember ordering honey barbecue wings, fries, and pineapple juice. He ordered a dinner special with a soft beverage. While we were eating, he moved his plate and cup out of the way for the waiter.

Tyler started telling me to pack up my personal belongings. He told me that we were going to have a conversation with my mom, and it needed to be done by the end of the month. I was blown away that he wanted to take the initiative to speak with Dorsey. He did not even know her at all. I was not sure if I wanted him to even see my mom, plus I was not really feeling comfortable with seeing Dorsey after how everything went down. Yet, I had nothing to lose at this point since he insisted on taking the lead role.

The day before I moved out of the Chad's home, I told the person I was leaving, and they respected my decision to leave on good terms. The following day in the early morning, I met Tyler in downtown Lancaster, and I got inside of his car. Afterwards we drove to Chad's home, to start putting my personal belongings inside his motor vehicle and then drove straight to Dorsey's house.

We arrived in the parking lot waiting for her to get back home. She pulled up and noticed me and Tyler. As soon as as she got out of her car, she looked very confused as to why me and Tyler were there. He told me to let him do all of the talking.

Tyler and Dorsey started talking for almost an hour and a half. I could hear deep conversations about oldies music, dance moves, laughs, and much more. I was just sitting on a lawn chair waiting patiently like someone does in the emergency room. They just kept talking non-stop about life, meanwhile I was not sure if their conversation was going to end.

Once the conversation started dying down, Tyler gave me a slight look in his eye, and that was when I knew he was going to talk about his testimony. I could already see him ready to open up and speak with complete openness. He went so deep into opening up his heart, Dorsey believed every word he said, and life was starting to look different for everybody at that moment.

Once Tyler gathered himself up with composure, he drove away in his car. He pretty much left me and Dorsey by ourselves to talk.

Once we started talking it was about my living arrangements. She asked if I ever stayed at the Water Street Mission; I said no I never did. I was allowed back inside my mom's home, but there was still tension between us, since she never wanted to have the real talk about our damaged foundation.

While I was living there I kept my distance from her, slept on the couch, left the home often, and focused on myself. The experience of me being homeless did cause me to mature in different areas of my life. I never turned to drugs, alcoholic beverages, or crime.

You may have seen people panhandling on the streets with signs trying to convince people to support their dysfunctional habits. The thought of me panhandling never crossed my mind because money was not even worth considering. I never was caught up on the wrong side of the law.

I got myself into being homeless due to a factor of choices I made and being set up for failure by Dorsey. Overtime I got myself out of being homeless and into my own apartment with my cousins Tony and Orlando. I'll talk about me and my cousins moving in together later on. The next time I left my mom's home it was on my own terms. There was no goodbye or farewell conversation with one last hug. I had grown so used to the lack of communication from my parents on things that needed to be addressed, that I just did not even bother starting that conversation at all. My transition of leaving my mom's home was a long time coming and ended without proper closure from my mom.

You may be asking where my dad was during my time of being homeless. He knew all about me going to court several times, facing eviction, eventually being homeless, and then getting out of homelessness. I remember him saying in one of our rare phone calls that he knew I would end up getting kicked out of my mom's home ever since I was a teenager. He later told me, in case the eviction took place, to be ready for the Sheriff to change the locks on the doors. My mom will never admit that what she did was wrong.

Arnold's statement was right because ever since I was a teenager, my mom would call him on the phone making false complaints about me, while she was the person causing and allowing all of the chaos to happen inside the household with my second step dad John and other family members. After that brief conversation with my dad, we had stopped communicating for some time.

Looking back now, I have come to realize estranged fathers hurt themselves by allowing a damaged relationship with a child to become worse. It can get to the point of not knowing how to come back from so many bad choices, from the many hearts broken, and after countless times of letting them down.

I originally was debating to myself if I even wanted to open up about my journey of being homeless, to getting out of being homeless, and getting an apartment. This was not the first time I actually faced being homeless or evicted. In the late summer of 2001, when I was a teenager, there was a time when the Sheriff actually did change the locks to the doors, put a special device to prevent the windows from being opened, and a colored paper on the front and back doors.

I recall being with my siblings and my mom to visit a distant cousin Tammy. This visit turned out to be something I did not see coming at all. An exchange of money had taken place with Dorsey and Tammy. After we left to drive back to our home, I noticed the sheriff and officers were right outside the home.

My mom had paid the judgment in full to the property manager, and the eviction was called off at the 11th hour. She never told me she was behind on the rent and had gone to court. I had no idea this was taking place until the last minute.

She was not going to tell me what just took place. I knew something was not right based on seeing how this situation was looking, and it involved the law again. I just had a hard time wrapping my mind on how she could allow this to happen to the family. With that being said, I realized my personal experience with being homeless and facing eviction relates to other people in America and around the world.

There have been plenty of success stories from people experiencing homelessness and evictions. I suppose you can say I am one of those success stories that hits home. I never gave up during this situation at all. This was just a transition point in my life that showed the foundation I was standing on. There was no sign while I was in recovery to show I would experience homelessness, use my legal rights to testify against Dorsey in court, and have this comeback remarkable comeback story.

Now I see why this old saying truly hits home all over the world. “A family that prays together stays together.” I was seeing Dorsey often in the hospital, rehab, and at home, but we never prayed together or had a serious conversation about the damaged relationship we have. You may find it very sad and be blown away.

Keep in mind a serious conversation cannot be forced, or this situation becomes combative and full of conflict. Now what can be done once a person is leaving an abusive relationship starts with setting up reasonable boundaries, keeping a distance from the individual, and giving a firm ultimatum.

I remember as I was starting to make progress from my health and passed the feeding test, my life was starting to look brighter and clearer. Then I get a text from my stepmom Hannah. She wanted to meet me for lunch on a Saturday morning. She picked me up at the Conestoga View nursing home's front entrance. Afterwards, we rode to the restaurant, enjoying the food and drink. Suddenly, out of nowhere, she dropped a bomb on me.

Hannah dropped a bomb on me by say "Your dad won't be helping you get your life back together." Just when I thought my life was getting better, it was a serious blow to be told this bad news. I just do not understand how somebody could be willing to tell me something so harsh when I was still in the reconstruction phase of my life. I am sure she would not want anyone she truly cares about to hear something like that.

I suddenly lost my appetite, realizing Hannah allowed herself to be used as a messenger by my dad, content to be the submissive wife. I did not see it coming at all. It was a completely horrible surprise. After we left the restaurant, I told her to drop me off at Manheim Township High School for a basketball game.

I enjoyed speaking with people at the game and reconnecting. It seems like sports have been my savior during my adversities and have helped me channel the energy constructively. As I was watching the basketball game, a group of older men spoke to me. I later found out, one of the older men was actually my cousin Phil.

Moving forward, the reality is my dad had been showing up at the hospital and rehab, seeming to be concerned for my health. He eventually went back to being an estranged father all over again once I started to get better with my health.

He received news that my health was better and that gave him the green light to go back to being distant all over again. After that day, I knew I had to go on with my life without him, but that was not going to stop me from continuing my journey of regaining everything I had lost.

If a person's heart does not change for the better neither does the intentional damage to future relationships.

My life started getting better and progress was being made. In the summer of 2012, I became a volunteer at the Teen Haven Camp, and I gave my testimony. At the camp, I was playing sports and games with the teenage kids and realized that my body had gotten stronger. My speed was back, and I felt naturally athletic for the first time in over a year. I remember feeling optimistic and acknowledged that I had gone from losing everything to feeling back on track.

Next on my list of personal achievements was to pass my driver's test. I received help from several people. Although it took me three tries to pass the driving test, I was overjoyed and felt proud that I was finally a licensed driver. Being behind the wheel was very life changing, as I was finally able to do things on my own time. While it brought me praise, it also caught the attention of people asking for rides. I had to let some people down so that I could keep growing and value my own time.

It took a full year to recover physically, mentally, and emotionally. I was still experiencing pain in my body and frequent headaches. I had to keep using medicine to cope once I passed my feeding test and consumed solid food again.

I noticed my body was transforming with more stability in my walk, better speech, and strength. I was no longer taking prescribed medicine and I could walk farther distances without stopping. Eventually, I would feel like going for a jog and end up doing a sprint. One day the sprint became very fast, and that was when I knew my athletic ability came back for good.

Once I was hired at the School District of Lancaster After School Sports Programs, attending Harrisburg Community College, and driving a car, there were plenty of people that were proud of the progress I made in my life. On Saturday, March 19th, 2011, my life changed forever. Every year that passes I give honor and glory to God on social media because he gave me a second chance at life, endless opportunities, and a purpose to fulfill.

When I spoke about my personal experiences at Teen Haven Ministries for the first time in front of the youth. I was so filled with humility that I needed time to regroup myself.

As the years started passing on, for each anniversary I would have somebody create a poster for me, and I would take several pictures to post on social media. It was both fun to celebrate, as well as a humbling experience. I was stepping out of my comfort zone to show a more authentic life.

I could have taken the easy route by posting a statement with a picture as I usually did on social media, but sometimes the easy way is not the best choice for things like my walking living miracle anniversaries. I felt like I could do more since so many people were proud just seeing me live my life productively.

For my ninth-year anniversary I decided to give it a voice. I made a short YouTube video to say, "I am a walking living miracle by the grace of God." It was totally different from just posting a picture and statement as my status on social media grew. The video was viewed by people from around the world using Facebook, Instagram, TikTok, YouTube, LinkedIn, and Snapchat. The shares, comments, and compliments were very positive responses.

I took a big leap of faith trying something new in my life. This was totally different from what I normally posted on social media. By doing this, it led to me doing more recorded special speeches and acknowledging the moments where I truly shined. There is no better feeling than me telling my own stories and speaking my own narrative. There was absolutely nothing holding me back from speaking my mind.

Giving honor and glory to God on social media creates a sense of humility, courage, and humbles my heart. I show people a different side of me besides the positive pictures, quotes, videos, and inspiration. You get to see the real me outside of being at a sporting or musical event. What you see is a young man saved by mercy and grace.

The activities seen on social media are normally a positive highlight reel of a person's life. From my life you have an opportunity to see the long journey I have overcome. There are very few people who truly show what God has done for their life. I found a purpose to use the anniversaries for the greater good.

In 2013, when I started getting noticed for what I overcame in my life, I realized I have a platform to use to inspire other people on Earth. I remember seeing how people I looked up to use their platform, such as Earvin "Magic" Johnson, Lebron James, Alicia Keys, Michael Jordan, Deion Sanders, and Steve Harvey. It started with people who I can relate to in my life. That is when I noticed I can relate with student-athletes and local leaders. I am a former student athlete, and I have great leadership skills that can be used for the greater good.

The first person who told me I inspired them was Diante Cherry, a three-sport star at J.P. McCaskey High School. He is the only male student-athlete to have one thousand yards receiving in football and scored over one thousand points in basketball. From there it led to many more student-athletes in Pennsylvania such as Allura "The Bunny" Blake, Ciara “CiCi" Long, Malia Taylor, Eli Washington, Devin Washington, Jameire Gray, Aniah Washington, Nick Allen, Naomi Gonzalez, Stenid Manning, Ariel Jones, Zaniah Banks, Tyler Crespo, Janeah Neal, Zakee Sailsman, Brianna Perry, Keenan Owens, Aaron Swinton Jr., Jada Turner, Katie Bushong, Elili Ayana, Marlia Matters, McKenzie Matters, Ciana Blake, Destiney McPhaul, Diamond Johnson, Sierra Bermudez, Kayla Bock, Stacy Summers, KiKi Jefferson, Andrew Williams, David Martin-Robinson, Nathan Henderson, Anthony Deleon, Nicte Machado-Aco, Sunshine McCrae, Jaylin Moore, Kassidy Ingram, Ava Stevenson, Robert Footman Jr., Jhamir Brickus, Dapree Bryant, Ricky Ortega, Tommy Ortega, Matt Ortega Jr. (aka Buggy), Nevaeh Acosta, Jeriyah Johnson, Aaron Young, Avery Young, Alyssa Schriver, and many more.

In the spring of 2019, I met a man named Kevin Hines, a walking living miracle for jumping over the Golden Gate Bridge and surviving. I heard about his story on YouTube. I was very grateful to see him speak at Millersville University. I experienced hearing him speak in-person and got to take several pictures with him. He was thankful to know my story as another walking living miracle. To inspire people can be a gift and purpose when used with the right intentions.

I can only be grateful for how many more anniversaries will come because you never know when the last one may be. I do value each of my anniversaries as they pass. I get to see the importance of living a life that is productive.

The opportunity to inspire people is showing that God can deliver miracles faster than an Amazon Prime package. The hospital is a place of facing reality away from social media with less distractions. You can see, breathe, sense and feel the energy once a miracle is completed. It is very remarkable and extraordinary in life itself as the impossible become the possible.

If you know where to look, you will see God's presence inside the operating room, delivery room, fire department, Intensive Care Unit, on every ambulance ride, and written in every police report. The purpose of a miracle is to show that adversity and hardship can be overcome. The miracle has produced results with added value in my life for being a supernatural moment that had been manifested by God.

Chapter 7. Furthering my Education

I remember finding myself back at Meadia Heights Golf Club attending an event, still on a feeding tube and severely underweight, and being greeted by people.

As the crowd sat down at their tables, I noticed Jordan Steffy looking my way. Jordan had started his speech then he waved his hand for me, calling me up into the spotlight, and the center of attention. I did not know why I was being called up in front of everyone. This situation was truly unrehearsed, instead it felt like an improvised play from back when I was on the football field.

With Jordan's hand around my shoulder, he made a very emotional speech, leaving people with tears in their eyes, and touching their hearts. I only remember him saying to the audience, "I believe Ethan will graduate college with a degree." I was shocked, thinking "how can he say that about my life while I'm still severally underweight and on the feeding tube?" I guess in his dreams and prayers, he saw something of what I would achieve in my life.

He must have been praying really hard to see that vision for my life. At that time, all I saw was my present state of adversities and dear hardships. Here I was barely able to walk around, not able to consume food, and living on liquids. That created a lot of pressure to make this type of statement in front of donors, sponsors, and many more people. I hope he was not trying to add pressure on me to get better, or maybe it was just his way of giving words of encouragement.

Looking back now, I'm shocked he even made that statement in front of the large crowd. That must have been the moment he professed and spoke it into existence. Once I finally passed the feeding test at Lancaster General Hospital, Jordan Steffy and his family were ready to take me out to eat for lunch and dinner. As I started gaining weight, my body went through a big transition and transformation. Life began to seem better once I had the feeding tube pulled out of my stomach.

At the time, I just did not see myself going to college. I did not see myself in higher education, touring college campuses, or graduating with a bachelor's degree. It was hard seeing brighter days ahead with the uncertainty of my recovery and health, doubting that I would ever make an honest living or even consume solid food again.

I remember the day a man named Luke tried to discourage me from pursuing college. He clearly did not believe in me and had no support to offer. He was trying to persuade me to work a normal dead-end job. I will tell him to look at me now; I am a college graduate with two degrees and turning my dream into reality.

I did not allow Luke's words to stop me from filling out the college application and doing a placement test. Sometimes in life we need to prove people wrong and have them eat their own words. That can be the motivator to go harder in life as the progress is being made. Hopefully he saw me on the front page of the Lancaster Newspaper and the WGAL feature of my inspirational story. I hope he saw that my testimony and productive progress went viral across the world, social media, communities, and people of all walks of life.

My next personal goal was to attend college. I was invited by Jordan Steffy to go on a college tour so that I could be exposed to different college choices. We visited Temple, Drexel, the University of Pennsylvania, Columbia, Princeton, Maryland University, Howard University, and many more college campuses.

During this time, I moved to a new apartment with my cousins in Lancaster city. We moved out on our own and found a three-bedroom apartment. I felt like a new man on this journey working towards completing my personal goals.

There was a job offer in the School District of Lancaster Athletic department. I knew the Athletic Director and most of the staff. I accepted the position for football, which led to me doing basketball, and track. At the same time, my application for enrollment to Harrisburg Area Community College was approved. I enrolled for three classes and started right away. Life was falling into place and my hard work was really paying off.

While I started attending Harrisburg Area Community College, it became a life-changing experience. I had not been in a classroom setting in several years and riding the Red Rose Bus Transportation was a humbling situation. I am thankful because at the time college students were not being charged for riding the bus round trip directly on the Lancaster Campus. I still remember those two buildings, hundreds of parking spots, walking trails, and tall trees. The campus was patrolled around the clock by highly-trained security officers.

I enjoyed arriving early in the morning on campus to do my work, sitting through long lectures, receiving help from the tutors, and visiting the college professors during their office hours. The tuition rates were very cost-effective and affordable for students. I saw people that were older than me trying to further their education. There were students coming from several different high schools enrolled through the Dual Enrollment program which allows juniors and seniors to take classes to earn college credits.

There were hundreds of people on the campus. I realized it was very convenient for the two buildings on campus to be very close together. No real threats took place that I am aware of, and I do not recall any serious drama. Everything was within walking distance with free parking (with my pass), a café downstairs in the main building, a fitness room, piano, and science labs inside the second building.

While I was on campus at HACC, nobody knew I was a walking living miracle at all. I was basically flying under the radar without a GPS tracker. I could be myself without the attention of people knowing my story, and this allowed me to focus on furthering my education freely. I made sure my work was completed ahead of time before leaving the campus for work. There was no use waiting until the last minute and rushing through the assignments.

While most things in my life were going well, I soon found myself back in court to fight against two different landlords who had been corrupt and tried to get more money out of me. The first suit was against a landlord who had said she was taking money out of our security deposit for alleged damages after we decided to not renew our lease.

Beverly sent pictures of the bathroom, countertop, living room, and alleged that we had damaged something. I quickly realized that the pictures she sent were not even from our apartment, which turned out to be from another random apartment that I had never seen. One picture that really stood out was a picture of a cast iron tub, inside of it was a yellow rubber ducky. I know that sounds very funny. (It makes me think, what grown man actually bathes with a yellow rubber ducky? I am thinking Shrek, the man from blue clues, or bob the builder). I caught myself laughing too hard to actually believe Beverly would send these pictures from another apartment.

My family members got a big laugh out of it and she admitted being sorry for sending the wrong pictures. I soon realized once the check never arrived and the deadline passed, it was time to take legal action.

The first check she wrote for the security deposit was late and a lawsuit was filed against Beverly. Tony decided to hold on to the check instead of cash or deposit into his account. That decision really held up receiving my part of the security deposit.

Me and my family members were waiting patiently inside the lobby before the courtroom hearing. This was our first time meeting our landlord in person. I was just surprised that Beverly was not willing to admit she was in the wrong.

Once the bailiff called everyone inside the courtroom, it was time to handle business and prove our case against the landlord. Since the landlord failed to mail the check within thirty days, Beverly had no legal rights to countersue or claim damages.

The judge was very impressed with how we testified and presented the evidence. The landlord had no real defense. Beverly was truly humbled by the judge once he mentioned he did not care about her flying in an airplane. He asked her to show the envelope of the check, but she was not able to provide anything.

The judge ruled in our favor we won the first case against Beverly. One hour later my Tony texted me to let me know the first check the landlord wrote before the civil claim was written from a closed account and was bad. We tried to work with her to write a replacement check, but she refused to do so.

Turns out the law states that a check that is written must be good for at least one hundred-eighty days or six months. Beverly even sent a text confessing to writing a bad check and did not plan on making things right. She paid the judgment with money orders so we could not trace her new bank account.

I ended up filing a second lawsuit against my landlord by myself. This time she agreed to be served electronically by email through my lawyer. After several delays of motions being filed, a court date was set up and court ordered mediation. After she refused to settle out of court, I ended up driving all the way down south to Atlanta, Georgia by myself on I-95.

The drive was very far, I had to call off work, and tell the college professors to excuse my absence from classes due to an out of state court date. I remember driving pass former slave plantations, gas stations, motels, and several state lines. Once I finally arrived at the court office in Atlanta, I was ready to take care of business. I was thinking to myself that it would be a long time coming for my landlord.

I remember going through the metal detectors and being patted down by the law enforcement. Afterwards, I walked inside the big courtroom to see several people with their court cases on the calendar. Once it was my turn to speak with the judge, she mentioned it was better to meditate because there was going to be a winner and a loser. My lawyer approached Beverly one last time to work things out, yet she refused to make things right.

Once the court case started, I spoke the facts about the case by showing my bank statement for the bad check, and text messages. The landlord had no real defense for writing a bad check. The judge humbled her by stating she wrote the bad check, the law is clear this is a crime, and she ruled in my favor.

I had never seen a person that pissed off before in my life. I ended up waiting inside the lobby with the bailiff to make sure she was not waiting for me outside in the parking lot with southern hospitality.

Soon after, I was offered a lease agreement for my own apartment and I thought I knew my landlord Joe, until he refused to provide maintenance and repair services when they were clearly needed. I ended up withholding all the rent money into an escrow account. One day, I received a notice for summons to court for back rent, possession, and eviction.

I went to Mid Penn Legal Aid for a lawyer, and they took my case. I subpoenaed the housing code inspector to court and took pictures of the housing code violations. I testified against my landlord Joe and the judge told me to show my landlord the picture of the dead mouse and other housing code failures to his face. The judge asked, "Who's in charge of the property?". My landlord Joe said, "I am your honor." The judge replied, "You should have hired an exterminator the next day, not two months later." Afterwards the Judge told me to show the picture of the dead mice to Joe's face an additional time. Once again, the judge ruled in my favor, and I got to keep all of the rent money.

Overall, I stood my ground and won both my civil suits against the corrupt landlords. It was a great feeling walking out of the courthouse knowing justice was truly served for the greater good.

During my fall semester in 2017, I had a meeting with my adviser, and she informed me I had plenty of earned college credits to graduate from HACC. The look on her face was filled with excitement. She told me I had earned more than enough college credits to apply for graduation and transfer right away to a university.

Right away my advisor had me apply for the graduation ceremony. She made a few calls and everything was set in place. I had no idea my hard work was paying off as I was feeling good about myself.

The ball was left in my court to find a university that can accept me as a graduate transfer student. I started looking into the following colleges in Pennsylvania: Franklin and Marshall College, West Chester University, Millersville University, Temple University, Drexel University, Messiah College, Central Penn College of Harrisburg, and the University of Maryland.

I finally experienced the feeling of knowing it was time to order the proper cap and gown and that my special moment would finally happen once I arrived at the Giant Center. There were a few people I had told about the graduation, and they were very proud of me.

The day of my graduation ceremony, I was working a 10-hour shift at a warehouse in Ephrata. The clock was ticking away as I could not wait to leave work right away once the shift was over. There I was built up with excitement as I was telling my co-workers about my special day. They were very happy for me as I was getting ready to finally clock out of work. Once it was time to leave I started driving for an hour to the Giant Center and barely made it on time.

After I parked my car inside the parking lot, I started putting on my cap and gown before I walked through the metal detectors. Once I walked through without any disturbance, the ushers led me right away to the proper area for seating, and handed me the ceremonies program. I started seeing plenty of students that I knew and people in the crowd.

I was accompanied by Jordan S. Steffy and George Veronis, who were there celebrating my achievement in the crowd. They were both super happy for me and really proud. We enjoyed this great moment together by taking pictures and going out to eat following my ceremony.

My mood was on a happy cloud knowing I was going to cross the finish line and become a college Graduate from Harrisburg Area Community College. Following my graduation from HACC, I realized I could transfer to Millersville University to officially complete my college education.

In December 2017, the moment of truth came once I applied to Millersville University. The paperwork had been filled out and faxed over to the Millersville University Transfer Coordinator. A fee for my official transcripts was paid by me. I was hoping my first choice as a graduate transfer student would truly pay off.

The letter from Millersville University finally came in the mail. I was very excited to see what the news was going to be for my future. Once I opened it up, I received my approved transfer letter to attend Millersville University. The letter in the mail stated I was approved as a graduate transfer student.

The campus at Millersville University is much bigger with several department buildings, more surveillance cameras, several parking areas, dorms, off-campus housing, and student activities. Students were always inside the library, Student Memorial Center, gym, and the dorms. I did not have the time or resources to be more involved on campus since I was working two jobs off-campus.

I majored in their communications program; I knew plenty of the staff, students, and alumni. Millersville University allowed me the opportunity to maintain my after-school sports programs job and stay close to home.

I thought about trying out for the Millersville University Men's football team as a walk on and joining the Millersville University TV club. I really wanted to play football again, this time on the collegiate level. I had already imagined wearing the black and gold football equipment. I was thinking about playing wide receiver, slot, return man, or cornerback.

I kept on dreaming from the time I was a former student-athlete in middle school and freshman year of high school. Then, a moment later, I had to be more realistic about my life and health. The thought of injury risk was on my mind. I could not afford to have a sports related injury to cause a delay in making sure I graduated with a bachelor's degree.

On the collegiate level, it is grown men playing and practicing the game of football against each other. I already saw players seeing the trainers for bumps, bruises, and serious injuries. This is a contact sport involving collisions. I still needed to work my two jobs to support myself and maintain a consistent work history. My journey was much different than most students since nobody knew I was a walking living miracle. So, I decided not to try out as a walk-on for the Millersville University Men's football team.

The risk to my health outweighed everything, and my dream of playing collegiate football was an afterthought compared to it. Thankfully, later on, Head Coach J.C. Morgan and his staff allowed me to attend a football game from the sideline with the team and enter the locker room.

The experience was everything I can reflect on to this day. I may not have put on the football jersey, pads, and mouth guard again.

However, I did walk away knowing it was worth at least considering taking the chance to live the dream before I hung up the cleats for good. I really wanted to play football again, this time on the college level. It just wasn't meant to be at that time, and I had already made the transition to working the football games and inspiring the future generations of student-athletes.

I have influenced plenty of student-athletes in several sports. I guess it was meant for me to still be involved in sports, just in a more behind-the-scenes type of role.

Millersville University TV helped college students earn more experience, visit television studios, jump start their careers, and build connections. The students would prepare stories about the weather reports, events, and other topics. They made reels for their professional job resume to carry around on flash drives and gain more exposure.

As for me, I had to work two jobs while attending both Harrisburg Area Community College and Millersville University. There was no financial support from family members. However, I did qualify for Pell Grants and PHEAA Grants, while my personal expenses had to be paid by me. That is why I did not join Millersville University TV.

I can only imagine that maybe I could have been hired in the television industry instead of working on my Ethan A. Poetic, LLC business. Sometimes the timing works and sometimes it just does not. Life will always go on as time keeps moving forward. I still manage to make my life work while facing the odds. I suppose living in poverty gave me an open-ended mindset to keep going until I finish the task.

I arrived on the campus with an appointment to meet with Dr. Theresa Russell-Loretz. She was very polite in helping me choose my classes as a transfer graduate student. I had a fun time working with Lisa in the business writing class. We used to stay up late at night researching for our assignments, typing out rough drafts, and complemented each other well.

Since I drove a Honda Civic, she was usually the passenger as I drove her to do errands, back to the college campus, and into Lancaster city. She helped me learn how campus parking works, how to improve my writing skills, and how to reserve a study hall room.

I surprised her with a lot of food one evening after completing a survey study for a company. The food was mostly dairy, and it did not go well with my allergy. As the college semester was ending, she ended up graduating from Millersville University.

Right before she took the Amtrak train back home to Philadelphia. She was very happy to see me again. As I was driving the car, I took the time to show her several areas of Lancaster. Eventually, she went on her way to China for work.

I was approved for an internship worth six credits and needed to complete two hundred and forty hours. I did over twenty interviews, traveling on the road, and meeting people with different experiences that have allowed me to share their stories and tell their own narrative.

This was a mighty task to achieve during the fall 2020 semester. I had to use my creative thinking to brainstorm how to best present everyone's story and use time management. For most of the people I interviewed we usually took pictures, and I gave them a thank you card as a token of my appreciation. I wore a suit for every interview, looking very sharp and professional, taking pride in my appearance, and making the most of each opportunity.

My time at Millersville University was very good with being safe on campus, getting my work completed ahead of time, connecting with new people, and creating positive memories. The campus life was usually full of diversity, unity, and opportunities. I remember the tutors really being a great resource helping me with my math assignments and exams. The professors were very welcoming, consistent with replying back to emails, communicate during office hours, and allowed students to earn bonus points. When I first moved to Lancaster I didn't think I would be graduating from HACC and Millersville University. I was just a teenager from Coatesville adjusting to a new environment in Lancaster. Even with the adversities I was facing in my life, I still managed to overcome them, and turn it into a success story to inspire the entire world.

While I attended these schools, nearby Franklin and Marshall College provided me with an eye-opening experience both on and off the campus. I remember waking up one day deciding to go visit Lancaster's Buchanan Park, just for fun. While I was there, I noticed hundreds of college graduates, their family members, and staff. A commencement ceremony was happening. I saw hundreds of students become college graduates, watching them cross the finish line.

As they say, the joy on their faces was priceless while I watched them pose for pictures with their family and classmates. The following year, I attended another Franklin and Marshall College graduation ceremony. This time was much more different since it was inside the Alumni Sports Fitness Center.

As I was walking through the aisles, a young woman was waving her hand at me. I walked over to her and she told me to sit with her in the front row. That was something I did not see coming at all. A few minutes later, a Franklin and Marshall College professor named Dr. Robby Mason sat next to me. He initiated a conversation and we soon hit it off. The professor gave me his contact information and invited me over to his home for a special gathering.

Once I arrived at his home, he introduced me to his victorious wife Mrs. Mason. She had made plenty of food ready to be served for dinner and dessert. Once more people started showing up to gather around the table for prayer. The conversations were very enlightening and refreshing, speaking on a variety of topics. There was plenty of laughter added in during the story telling.

As we gathered inside the living room to share a song, poem, and their playing of musical instruments, the vibe was climbing to higher levels as everything was very genuine and authentic. The first impression really counted as I continued to come back for the experience for several years until a change of plans took place. I was able to meet and greet with college students that were leaders of the Black Student Union and other college campus groups. Those people welcomed me with open arms even though I was attending Harrisburg Area Community College and Millersville University.

They saw me for a man that was pursuing higher education and making the world a better place. I still remember meeting several of the Alumni who shared their experiences of facing discrimination. They explained how much had changed over the years thanks to continued support, federal laws being enforced, and passing of the torches to the future students. The impact on me was that previous college graduates had a much harder journey and they had to stay united through those circumstances. I fully understand why some people don't come back to the college they graduated from. They definitely allowed me to see from their perspective the importance of crossing the finish in the marathon.

I still remember my academic advisor, professors, classmates, staff, and tutors from Millersville. They helped me cross the finish line of passing the classes, completing assignments, and earning college credits, even when Millersville University's campus was shut down due to the COVID-19 pandemic. Thanks to the big transition towards online learning via Zoom, I still managed to do the work and put in the time to graduate.

I remember the day I filled out my application for graduation from Millersville in PDF format. The moment of filling out the paperwork and sending it back to my academic advisor was very exciting. Once my college credits and requirements were met at 100%, I knew it was time for a celebration that I had earned and deserved.

I hosted my own college graduation celebration with plenty of guests, food, soft beverages, and positive memories. I made sure everything was very simple and straight to the point. The parking lot had plenty of room for motor vehicles and was handicap accessible. I wanted to make sure that everyone I loved would be able to celebrate with me.

I did not cry when I gave my speech or when people started making awesome statements about me. We took plenty of pictures, the cake was cut into many pieces, and I received several gifts. I am presently a graduate of Millersville University, who majored in Speech Communications with a focus on Broadcasting & Media. I was planning on pursuing a career as a sports anchor, television host, daytime television personality, radio, and advocate speaker.

I had the plan of starting my television career in 2021, but I experienced rejection and had to rework my life plan. I started working for the School District of Lancaster as a Building Assistant and for spring track events. After the school year was over, I switched to working for the Substitute Teacher Service as a tutor, helping the students learn math, reading, and in the enrichment program.

Once a teacher learned of my story as a walking living miracle, she wanted me to tell the students my personal story during reading time. The kids gravitated to me asking for my autographs and to take pictures with me. They will always remember my story and cherish the memories. As for the teacher, she has a compassionate heart to have allowed the children in the summer program to feel truly inspired.

I never planned on telling those kids or the teacher my personal story. Again, with people having cell phones to research me, or anybody in general, on Google, Bing, Yahoo, or any internet search engine, it just happens. The pictures they see of my life on social media are real life experiences and very relatable to other people's journeys.

I have learned over the years to get used to everything. It is not that I ask for attention, compliments, praise, awards, or applause. I guess it is the energy and vibe being given off once people come into the same space as me.

During the summer of 2021, I ended up starting my own business called Ethan A. Poetic, LLC. My business involves me being a keynote speaker, life coaching, hosting poetry workshops, and entrepreneurship. I was able to have my website, domain, logo, design, and other things created by Sparrow Websites. They were very convenient to allow my vision to come alive through the website. The business cards were created by Staples and a married couple helped me with filling out the legal documents with the IRS and Harrisburg, Pa.

I was referred to Larry, under his guidance he taught me how to craft my message, story, travel with him to speaking engagements, and go through critique. He was a big help with showing me the ropes on the business side and telling me what I needed to hear. We shared plenty of laughs together about our stories. I was able to start speaking at elementary and middle schools. Larry would watch me from either the back row or in the front row, while I was center stage delivering my message to the kids.

I furthered my education with two college degrees and attended two commencement ceremonies. The celebrations will always be remembered for the rest of my life. Walking across the stage is a moment of joy to be cherished forever. Nobody can take my degrees away; Those were lifelong proud achievements. There is power in having the knowledge, wisdom, and common sense to be patient and make the right decisions. I believe in the importance of defending your honor, building a solid foundation, and adding value to your own life.

Everybody has a purpose for their life. Everyone is born with gifts and talents. In order for dreams to come true, you have to work for them all year round. Be surrounded by the right people who will help you become a better version of you. You can be a product of your environment, influences, and choices by your parents, guardians, adopted parents, or foster's parents. I believe it is totally up to you on an individual level whether you allow it to define or strengthen you.

Once you start making more positive decisions over negativity, adversities, and hardships, you will start to grow more and separate yourself from negative people. You will certainly outgrow and outwork some of the people that are in your life

---

Jason & Nicole McKinney, a married couple from church, helped me get my driver's license, and they were very happy for me. Once I passed the test, my emotions were joyous. I took a picture to post my achievement on social media and I got over a hundred likes and several comments. I then got my first car, with a title to a 1995 Ford Taurus as a starter vehicle. I was driving on the road in no time. The feeling of having my own car was freedom. No more waiting at the bus stop for transportation. I loved that Ford Taurus, but by May 2016, I knew it was time to get a different car, and I called a dealership about finding something better.

Since the Taurus was so old, it was time to let it go and move on as the wear and tear added up. By that time, I couldn't even drive it to find a replacement vehicle. I was told to find a way to the Apple Honda Dealership of York, and my friend Lisa to give me a ride. I offered her gas money, but all she wanted was a hot beverage to start the morning from the Lancaster coffee shop, Mean Cup.

Lisa was wondering what type of car I was getting. She had no idea, but I was getting a brand-new 2016 Honda Civic from the show room. Once we arrived at the dealership, I told her. The look on Lisa's face said "no way Ethan lol." Once she saw me test drive the red 2016 Honda Civic, Lisa was filled with excitement, joy, and pride. She brought out her cell phone to take pictures of me with the car. Then she sent the pictures to her friends and co-workers, putting me on blast in a positive way.

She still reminds me of that day all the time. That was a very exciting moment for me. I never in my life thought I would be driving a brand-new car out of the showroom. The process that got me to that moment was maintaining a high credit score, consistent work history, and knowing the right people. I did something most people did not envision me doing at all. It takes courage to get behind the wheel of a car after facing death the way I did.

The moment of truth had taken place in my life once my dad Arnold saw me in a brand new 2016 Honda Civic. I remember somebody saying go up to his home and show him what he missed out on. Instead I choose not to show up at Arnold's home or post anything on social media, I just let word of mouth travel back to Arnold. He must have been very proud of me for getting my driver's license and traveling on the road.

The point is, even though my dad sent his wife Hannah as a messenger to end our relationship, I was able to maintain my composure to not feel sorry for myself as a grown man. It's funny how the table turns as I was driving the brand-new Honda Civic down the streets of Coatesville. Once my dad saw me with the brand-new car; he was shocked and did not see it coming at all. I did something great without him. It is the journey towards success, not the destination of success

---

I have learned when you put in the work, sacrifices, time management, and consistent effort, your dreams will come true and become your reality. Keep doing the right things, live your life as you intended and cross the finish line. And when your life's coming attractions come true, they will be celebrated as they should be. The imagination is everything for the preview of life's coming attraction.

They say dreams are life's coming attraction for your future. I started out not knowing what my life was going to be when I was on my anticipated deathbed. While I was underweight on the feeding tube, there were times I was not sure if I would ever regain my freedom and independence again. Once I started regaining everything, I began seeing visions of my life's coming attractions. I was looking forward to living those dreams every day. Always remember your dreams can come true.

I was already taken off prescription sleeping medications. Going through the process of rehab was a humbling experience which included relearning how to speak correctly, walking, and regaining strength, confidence, dignity, and pride. I was used to not needing help or assistance to do the little things. As I look back on it now, the journey left me wondering if there was any end to the time and energy I would have to invest in attempting to regain what I lost from the car accident.

Being named a walking living miracle has been a blessing towards living a new life. Turns out it can be turned into inspiration, be motivational and uplifting. When I willingly put in the hard work, dedication, commitment, and made the most of help from people, the fruits of my labor started paying off. Not too many people saw it coming. Once I did exceed their expectations, I knew I got there by following a positive plan. My life started becoming more than hope, turning into an experience of justice and success.

Take a genuine look at me now, with a better quality of life, more opportunities, and significant grace. I went from being a passenger in a horrible accident to driving my own brand-new Honda Civic straight from the show room. I went from not working a job to completing an internship at a local television station and volunteering. I went from earning a high school diploma to earning my first degree from Harrisburg Area Community College.

In December 2020, I earned a bachelor's degree at Millersville University, majoring in Communication and minoring in Broadcasting and Media. The celebrations have been priceless. I did the impossible when the odds were against me. I did the unthinkable when life was on the rough side of the neighborhood. The older a person gets, the harder it is to further their education.

To be the first sibling out of 8 to graduate from both a Community College and University, it was such a high achievement, very honorable, and a proud highlight of my life crossing the finish line by ending the education chapter of my life on a sky-high note. Maybe I will go for both my master's and Ph.D. or Doctoral degree to raise the stakes even higher.

I am one of very few men on both sides of my family with two college degrees. I have a two second cousin's that have earned both a Master's and Doctoral degree. They had fulfilled the purpose for their lives.

As for my journey through college, I did not have a girlfriend. I remember the saying that a woman in a man's life can be his backbone to motivate him during his low points and keep him inspired to keep moving forward. I can say I did not do it with support from people that should have been there. Yet, when the foundation is fragile, it is best to create your own way and work with people that have your best interest at heart.

I am one of only a few men in my family that actually attended and graduated from college. My path was much different than most students in the USA. I did not have an athletic or academic scholarship. I relied on Pell and PHEAA grants to cover the cost of tuition and fees.

One of the most remarkable moments was repaying all of my college loans before I officially graduated from Millersville University. I deposited a large sum of money into my savings account and called the 800 number to pay the entire amount of the debt. That way I could start the 2021 New Year with no college debt and build up my credit score.

Chapter 8. Breaking the Cycle

To break the cycle of bad behavior patterns, we have to start with having an open-minded perspective. We must take an honest look at ourselves with courage and humility. Growing up, I saw the best things and the absolute worst things in life. I saw grown men in my neighborhood on Oak Street being active with the children, celebrating birthday parties, and being providers for their families. They allowed me to connect with their families through sports, video games, conversations, and being a true neighbor.

As a child, I grew up in poverty, and it was normal to me since I did not know what the difference was between being rich and poor. I did not grow up with many material things, the nicest sneakers, or eating at five-star restaurants. The days of eating at McDonalds, Wendy's, and Burger King were my "normal". I was born into poverty by default for living in a single parent household.

Breaking the cycle sometimes means going against the grain and the norms of negative behavior patterns that past generations settled into. There is a stage of growing apart from certain people that have bad intentions. A new behavior pattern can help usher in the future generations with a fresh start to their lives.

I have learned that breaking the cycle means to have the courage to go against the grain, family traditions, behavior patterns, and ways of thinking. Even though I saw people doing bad things and good things, I have a choice to do better or worse. I believe prayer can help break the poverty mindset which includes the language of poverty and its lifestyle.

Growing up with less can create a deep hunger for success. Poverty taught me to stretch what little money I had growing up. This habit allowed me to unknowingly think of budgeting my money and make it last for the long-term future. I can live for the moments, days, and weeks without going over my budget. It does not matter if people do not agree with my spending, saving, and investment habits. I have a life to live within my own means in order to maintain stability.

One of the life skills I have learned was how to cook by watching the Food Network channel. The television talents spoke in ways I understood without asking too many questions. Before I knew it, I was cooking in the kitchen while my mom came home from work. She ended up having me cook for the family, and the table was the gathering place for lunch and dinner.

The blessing was that I felt wanted inside the household. The curse was I was unknowingly filling a void I had no capacity to do as a child since my stepdad left. Without a father figure inside the household anymore me and my siblings had to do more things on our own.

A reality check is what some people often need to break the cycle, being shown the troubling effects it has on the family and future generations. For some people, it takes jail, death, a drug overdose, breakup, or a big loss to break the cycle and turn towards having a more purposeful life.

I have learned to never get drunk because it creates a very fragile position to be in, a vulnerable time of misjudgment. I have learned to never buy or use street drugs since it hurts the community, leading to gun violence, families being broken up, and addiction. The drug task force and law enforcement agencies collect forfeiture money from any person illegally dealing, distributing, or possessing drugs.

A person can always take it one day at a time to break the cycle by being around the right people to help them stay on the right path. The key is humility in knowing the real purpose for your life. Poverty can show who is being intentional about rising above those tough financial burdens. Welfare can help you in your time of need. Just do not get complacent, selling yourself short by settling for less.

The welfare system does not owe people anything, especially since welfare recipients rely on using taxpayers' money to be enabled. Always have an exit strategy with a mentor that is willing to show you the ropes. When you look back on your life, back to when you were in your twenties and thirties, there will be so many lessons to be learned and mistakes to move on from.

Breaking the cycle requires you to look honestly at your family history. No matter how much money you have, your mindset is what guides you. Dysfunction can happen in the poorest or the richest neighborhood. Not everybody that comes with you goes with you. Once you start breaking away from bad behavior patterns, you set yourself apart from the crowd.

You will start to outgrow some people and not everybody will be happy for you. It takes courage to stand alone and move away from the crowd. Once you have found the right crowd, you will see brighter days ahead. The right crowd leads to better opportunities for your life while you grow apart from negative people.

Leaving the crowd can mean leaving a gang, drug ring, job, home, jail, and unhealthy relationships. Distance is needed to get away from distractions and wrath. The people you are around the most are who you are likely to become. If you invest time in the library reading laws, history, and sports, your mind will grow in knowledge. The streets do not care about you, after all it is just a game that will lead to insecurity, prison, and death.

There are a few people I have seen turn their lives around by leaving the street life behind them. They have strong testimony to share, and hopefully they can change one life. Most people who choose the street life come from broken foundations. Other people doing blue- and white-collar crimes have bad intentions. They may come from a household that had a solid foundation.

For some reason the temptation to do things that seem beneficial but will only make their life worse takes them down a dark path. I know several people that have thrown their lives away, and the costs are limitless. They have experienced losses of marriages, businesses, custody of their children, homes, yachts, passports, airplanes, licenses, military status, and professional licenses. We sometimes do not know what we have until it is gone or taken away.

Never allow yourself to be pulled down from your success. People with bad intentions will suck you dry until you have nothing left to give willingly. If you have a vision of red flags, take it seriously and cut that person or group of people off. There is no good in carrying dead weight and slowing down your progress.

Most successful people keep their circle very small with assets, not liabilities. Most successful people keep tight to a schedule with time management by the hour not the day. Once you allow your gifts to make room for you, you will live a fruitful and blessed life.

In order to be successful in life, you need to be held accountable, acknowledge the whole truth, and take responsibility for your choices. The spotlight can be put on you as the leader that is in charge. Having the right people on your team will make everything much easier as growth is taking place.

Chapter 9. Clarity

I never asked, requested or prayed to become an inspiration and all of the attention that comes with it. I guess it is all part of the growing process, turning negativity into positivity. The process was not what I set out for as I started working again and enrolled into community college.

I started working in the community. Since I worked with children and student-athletes, I was researched by parents, guardians, and children on the internet.

The adults and youth were referred right back to my near fatal car accident by the news articles and television story about it. There was discomfort bringing it up at my job. I originally just wanted to enjoy relating to the student athletes, since I am a former student-athlete myself. That is how I was pushed to return through that pedestrian crosswalk, into the school zone, and back to calling the school building home.

I wanted to turn the attention I was receiving from my near fatal car accident around by having people focus on the positive in my life and how I have kept moving forward. I knew I had moved past it in my actions, but some people still wanted to keep the focus there. I can understand they may wonder how did I even survive the near fatal car accident head on against an 18-wheeler. The other side of the situation is parents and guardians want to know who the adults that are around the children.

There were turn back moments. I wanted to start giving recognition to student-athletes and local leaders as a turning point. The investment came back in return several times over for my 10th year anniversary.

Always clap for other people's achievements, honors, legacies, and milestones because you never know when it will be your turn to receive recognition. Now when I show up to work the energy and vibe that made me nervous at first is my comfort zone.

I am not a celebrity by any means at all. If I become famous around the world, it was meant to happen over time, doing something great to truly impact the world as lives are forever changed. As I was in Lancaster General Hospital, Lancaster Rehab, and spending five whole months on a feeding tube, I did not imagine my life would really transform to greater heights. My testimony exceeded footprint.

I recently went back to Lancaster General Hospital and Lancaster Rehab to be there in the present moment. I was once in the patient's shoes while on my journey. As I was there, the thoughts of being in a hospital bed did bring back some memories. The visitors would be waiting to speak with me in person and have genuine conversations. I no longer needed a wheelchair for me to be pushed in. I no longer needed to use the side bars to move.

The ambulance has become normal to me, hearing the sirens rushing to make an impact on a person's life. I made time to visit the scene of the near-fatal car accident to be in the moment as the motor vehicles drove by. My current life is more peaceful and has evolved over time several years moving forward.

The Ten-Year Anniversary as a Walking Living Miracle is a reflection of hard work, perseverance, grit, and determination. The dash on my headstone has not been created. Instead, there is still more time on earth for me to fulfill my purpose. I have been able to build relationships with people of all walks of life.

Chapter 10. Blessings, Awards, & Interviews

Several years ago, I did not see any positive life's coming attractions in the midst of my near-death experience. Since the people that were praying for me saw better days ahead in my life, they would visit me inside the hospital, rehab, and at my home.

One day which caused my life to change forever was when I received a passing grade for my math class and completed my internship at Lancaster Community Television Station Channel 66. College math was not my favorite subject, I just knew I needed to write out the steps to show all the work for credit. The Pre-Algebra, Survey of Mathematical Ideas classes were very challenging, and consumed so much of my free time. I was going to see the math professor during office hours, working with tutors, and writing notes all the time.

The internship was more challenging due to following COVID-19 protocols, wearing a mask and using hand sanitizer all the time. I was very fortunate to have the supervisor on board and approval from the Career Learning Center. I originally applied to do an internship at WGAL for the experience and to add to my resume, but it just did not work out that way. I did not hear back from anybody for a zoom meeting or a response to my application.

Being in the situation where I needed to cross the finish line during my senior year, I still needed more credits to qualify for both the PHEAA and Pell grants to cover the cost of my tuition and fees. My situation had to be figured out on a priority level before the deadline for the paperwork to be fully processed.

Once my internship was approved for Lancaster Community Television station channel 66, I started the process of scheduling the interviews right away. I contacted a lot of people and traveled much farther than usual to log in 240 hours. It took a lot of time management to keep track of those hours, my college math assignments, and working with the tutors.

I furthered my education with two college degrees and attended two commencement ceremonies. The celebrations will always be remembered for the rest of my life. Walking across the stage is a moment of joy to be cherished forever. Nobody can take my degrees away; Those were lifelong proud achievements. There is power in having the knowledge, wisdom, and common sense to be patient and make the right decisions. I believe in the importance of defending your honor, building a solid foundation, and adding value to your own life.

Everybody has a purpose for their life. Everyone is born with gifts and talents. In order for dreams to come true, you have to work for them all year round. Be surrounded by the right people who will help you become a better version of you. You can be a product of your environment, influences, and choices by your parents, guardians, adopted parents, or foster's parents. I believe it is totally up to you on an individual level whether you allow it to define or strengthen you.

Once you start making more positive decisions over negativity, adversities, and hardships, you will start to grow more and separate yourself from negative people. You will certainly outgrow and outwork some of the people that are in your life.

The interviews I have been featured on and conducted for my college internship are broadcasted on television 7 days a week. The experience of allowing stories to be told and narrated into their own words was very worthwhile. I am very thankful for the time and resources of people that have contributed to this area of my life.

This was an area where having good relationships paid off, as many people I had met over the years welcomed me into their homes and workplace for interviews. Coach Matt Ortega and his wife Corrie allowed me to interview their entire family. It felt great going back to my humble beginnings in Coatesville. I am very thankful for maintaining a strong connection with the Ortega family for several years.

I spoke to Dr. Todd Mealy for a very long time as we got into a comfortable conversation. We had talked about him attending Bishop McDevitt High School in Harrisburg, playing football, and his transitions to coaching football, becoming a teacher, and college professor.

I was able to interview Neumann-Goretti high school basketball player Sierra Bermudez and her mom Shannon Hyre Coatesville Area High School Alumni. Special thanks for the introduction from Mia Matuszewski, a childhood friend of mine from Coatesville, PA. She coached at Scott Middle girls' basketball team and hosted several basketball clinics. Mia built and maintains a great relationship with Sierra's family.

Shannon spoke about being truly committed to both of her children's success as student athletes, and doesn't consider it a sacrifice. The family support was consistent all year round, with traveling on the road, making reservations at hotels, and being involved with the fundraiser's events. There can be a lot of pressure on the relationships between a child and parents. Starting with being a fan first, parent, and making sure the goals are meant.

Shannon speaking from a parent's perspective goes into great details. There was a lot of traveling on the road with the Philadelphia Belles AAU basketball team on the weekends, building meaningful relationships, creating memories from those experiences. The challenges involved never taking the easy route in life.

Shannon made the decision to have her daughter transfer to Neumann-Goretti High School. Sierra was able to rise to the occasion for adjusting to a new school, program, teachers, coaches, team mates, and making new friends.

Sierra became the best version of herself as a positive student-athlete. Sierra was able to earn a full ride athletic Scholarship at Clarion University. She spoke about being thankful for being pushed by her coaches to build her confidence, shooting ability, and working consistently hard to be her very best. I can tell Sierra was truly committed to putting in the work when nobody was looking.

She was working on mastering her craft with a personal trainer and personal basketball trainer. By working on the little things to perfect everything and have positive results. She is thankful for using advanced technology tools or resources to increase her recovery time, to allow her body to fully heal. Basketball is a game that requires a lot of time on both indoor and outdoor basketball courts. The balance between fun and work is a must for having so much love for the game of basketball.

The interview took place in Caln Township, Pa at Caln Township Park. We were able to conduct the interview inside the pavilion. Sierra was making consecutive basketball shots while I was her ball boy under the rim, and her mom Shannon recorded everything from the sidelines. I believe it was natural chemistry as we all worked together to make an outstanding interview. I was there in person to see her sign on the dotted line to Clarion University. Sierra gave special thanks to her coaches, teammates, trainers, family members, and friends.

Nicte Machado-Aco, alumnus of J.P. McCaskey High School, special multi-talented student-athlete traveling student athlete, giving back to the community. earned a full ride academic scholarship. She mentioned taking I-B classes encouraging student's own way of thinking, addressing global issues, rigorous lectures, earning college credits, and earning a I-B Diploma. I was amazed at how she takes her education very seriously, by visiting college campuses, sitting in lecture halls, and being prepared for college ahead of time.

Nicte's natural athletic ability started with her passion and favorite sport for soccer. She made the varsity soccer team as a freshman and named the team captain. During her 12th grade year she couldn't play because she joined a traveling soccer team which prevented her from playing on the varsity soccer team. Nicte chose to play varsity football as a fall sport, she became the female kicker, she's first girl to score points from a field goal on the varsity boys football team, and made history.

During Nicte's freshman year she made the varsity indoor and outdoor track team, and served as a team captain. Even though Nicte had no previous track experience, she was committed to be coachable, committed, led by example, and created bonds with several of her teammates.

In the summer of Nicte's freshman year, she joined the Lancaster City track team; her, the coaches, and several teammates traveled to different locations to compete in competitive track meets. She played the clarinet for the J.P. McCaskey High School marching band, during both her tenth and eleventh grade year. I realized her hard work paid off to become the Vice-President of the National Honor Society. Nicte participated in and organized an event for “Relay for Life" to help raise money for cancer research.

Her parents are huge advocates for academics, and making sure Nicte strives to do her very best. She’s very thankful that her parents were involved with the fundraiser events, senior night events, attending the sporting events, and kept her motivated all year round.

Ethan Poetic supports and inspires Nicte Machado- Aco J.P. McCaskey High School three Sport Star Student Athlete. Nicte is born with many gifts and talents. She not only competes in soccer, Varsity football, Varsity Track and Field.

She wears many hats by being active in Vice President of National Honor Society, State Medalists in Track and Field, Penn Relays, Junior Olympics, Lancaster City Track Club, and involved in many clubs at her high school.

She’s a proud Latina positive Leader, and Captain of three Varsity Sports. She plays on a traveling soccer team called Pa Classics Da. She did participate in the Senior Homecoming. Nicte does play Music in the High School Band. She does sing and of course is bilingual in both English and Spanish.

Nicte is the first and only girl to score points on Varsity Football for J.P. McCaskey High School. After graduation this upcoming June 2019. Nicte plans on furthering her education to study premed and become a Cardiothoracic Surgeon meaning help people with heart and health problems. She also plans to play Soccer on the Collegiate level.

Nicte Machado-Aco

J.P McCaskey High School

Class of 2019

Nevaeh Acosta is an alumnus of J.P. McCaskey High School, earned a full ride academic scholarship to Penn State. During my interview with her, I learned she's bilingual in both English and Spanish to use that as a competitive advantage for her career and networking. She enjoyed having the college feel while enrolled in dual-enrollment classes, opportunities to connect with students from other high schools, and college professors.

Nevaeh participated in several years of gymnastics with the events such as; uneven bars, floor exercise, parallel bars, horizontal bars, pommel horse, vault, and the balance beam. She earned the honor of being named a four-time state champion. I learned gymnastics takes a lot of determination, serious commitment, and endurance.

Nevaeh made the varsity indoor and outdoor track teams. She went on to compete in both middle distance and relay teams' events. During her free time, she joined the gospel choir to sing praise and worship songs.

Nevaeh's mom influenced her to try as many things as possible at a young age. Her mom encouraged her to take education very seriously to have more opportunities. She saw that her mom did make a great impact into the lives of hundreds of children both as an educator and cheerleading coach.

During the High School Commencement ceremony, Nevaeh served as the Class President, and she cherished giving her heartfelt speech. I can personally say she definitely set the bar high for her younger siblings and led by example. Her parents were always there to make sure Nevaeh and her siblings experienced agape love and appreciated it.

Malia Taylor is an alumnus of J.P. McCaskey High School; she earned a basketball athletic scholarship at Bloomsburg University. I first saw Malia play sports and do choir at Lincoln Middle School. During her time at J.P. McCaskey High School. She went on to play competitive AAU basketball, four years of Varsity Basketball, and varsity Track as a runner, high jump, and long jump.

Malia was named into a leadership role as a team captain, showing other teammates the right way to play the game, provide guidance, and make sure they do their classwork on a priority level. She's very thankful of her coaches and trainers providing the support behind the scenes. She mentioned the I-B program helped with preparing for college, challenging classes, and building connections with the professors. She went on to earn extra college credits through the dual-enrollment program. Her mom was very supportive with the carpooling, fundraiser events, and cheering her daughter and teammates at the sporting events.

Elili Ayana is an alumnus of J.P. McCaskey High School. She speaks English, Amharic, Amharic, Oromo, and Spanish. She felt like it was a second home with the Gospel Choir singing praise and worship songs.

Elili made both the varsity indoor, and outdoor track teams as a mid-distance and long-distance runner. She was competing on the Lancaster City Track club during the summer season. Elili loved that her family supported her with sports, music, and education. She felt motivated to keep a strong work ethic all year round and set the right example for the youth that looks up to her.

Ciara Long aka CiCi is an alumnus of J.P. McCaskey High School, bilingual in both English and Spanish languages to communicate with more people. Ciara had a wonderful experience in the dual enrollment program to earn college credit at Harrisburg Area Community College. She made the varsity girls soccer team and bowling teams, volunteered for unity track, enjoyed senior night celebrations with her family, and made a lasting impression with her wonderful teachers.

She was influenced to do soccer by her parents and found a passion for the sport. While being the team captain was very fun and helping out the team mates. Ciara experienced a transition into womanhood through her sweet-sixteen celebration. The ceremony had a prayer, father-daughter dance that became a cherished moment between Ciara and her dad.

During her time helping out kids with special needs, she encouraged others to do their very best, and finish the track and field events. Her family is always there for each other for special events, celebrations, and maintaining consistent communication.

Allura "The Bunny" Blake is an alumnus of J.P. McCaskey High School. I remember when I first saw her as a team manager for the Wheatland track team. She was really engaged in mastering the high jump, long jump, and running techniques. During her seventh and eighth grade year, she made the girls basketball team and track teams. She went on to break both the high jump and long jump records at Wheatland Middle School.

While Allura attended J.P. McCaskey High School, she enjoyed her experience in the ROTC program aka Reserve Officer Training Corps. I remember she was wearing the military uniform, doing the marches, and was honored at a Varsity football game.

Allura went on to play both freshman and Junior varsity basketball. She was very competitive doing four years of varsity track and field. The decision was made by the coaches to have her start varsity track right away. By participating in the high jump, long jump, triple jump, and hurdles. That's how she earned the nickname "The Bunny" for her consistent jumping motions.

Allura's positive experiences at McCaskey High School are the opportunities for students, such as Dual-enrollment, AP Classes, I-B program, and much more. She's very thankful of her coaches, friends, teammates, trainers, mentor, and family. For being her rock, supportive, positive influences, always being there for her.

Dejon Manning is an alumnus of J.P. McCaskey High School; Kent State University earned an athletic scholarship for track. During Dejon's four years of varsity sports, he made a lasting impression on the indoor, outdoor, and Lancaster City Track teams. Dejon started off doing the hurdles, sprinting events, and relays. He had a consistent work ethic, named team captain, and helped break track records. The 4x4 relay team broke Black Knight Invitational, J.P. McCaskey High School and Lancaster-Lebanon League records.

Dejon embraced being the leader for his younger siblings, and leading by example in both education, athletics, and legacy. He was a host for the Arch assembly and put on a show for his solo flashy dance moves. He earned an I-B diploma for his hard work and determination.

Dave Burman is an alumnus of Strath Haven High School and York College earned a bachelor's degree. Dave and his family grew up in Chester, Pa until the family moved to Strath Haven School District. I remember seeing Dave doing the announcement at varsity football and basketball games. He's supported by his lovely Wife Brenda. Dave grew up in Chester, Pa until his family moved to Strath Haven School District.

I had contacted Dave for an interview request for my internship and Dave gladly accepted. I drove I-95 south to Chester High School. The location was very convenient to conduct the interview in front of the entrance. He went on to mention the facts about the City of Chester, High School Sports, and family history, and his professional career in radio.

Dave speaks about me being a walking living miracle and being amazed that I'm still alive with a great purpose. He was really surprised to see I'm the true definition of a comeback hero story. I didn't see that coming once he mentioned my personal story during the interview. He loved that I never gave up when I was facing serious adversities and a near death experience.

Dave and His Wife Brenda did treat me to Chili's for dinner. We took plenty of pictures, had a great conversation, and made a forever bond together.

Jada Turner is a current student-athlete at Manheim Township. She competes in Varsity girls' soccer and has won several gold medals.

She enjoyed seeing her older sister play varsity basketball at Lancaster Catholic High School. Her mom Jenine Turner is an alumnus of Manheim Township High School. Soccer and Track traveling team. I recall attending her eighth-grade promotion, she was really surprised to see me there. We took pictures together, and had them emailed to her mom right away.

Jenine recalls being involved in the carpool rides, fundraiser events, traveling on the road, and working together with the parents. She's very proud of both of her children succeeding in life, sports, education, and giving back to the community.

Jenine truly enjoyed cherishing those special moments to see her children at practices and games. Support your children all year round, learn the difference between being a fan and a parent. Those moments can't come back.

Susan Springsteen is an alumnus of Concord High School in Wilmington, Delaware, Wheaton College, and Entrepreneur. She's very good with numbers such as Calculus One, enjoys riding horses, and creating. As a teenager she realized the importance for women to earn at least a four-year degree, to move up in a career, and obtain success.

I remember her speaking about sacrifices to have a better long-term future and building a solid foundation. Susan enjoyed the corporate world for selling her services, she later on was able to create jobs for people with her own business, and help improve the communities.

Susan's proud achievements were during college when she changed her major from chemistry to business and economics. She ended up finding her purpose with her decision and graduated on time from Wheaton College. Susan remembers an old saying the day a person is born and the day a person finds out why. I remember Susan mentions, by leaving a true legacy through impacting other people for the greater good.

Susan had an unbelieve experience to be invited and visit the White House in Washington D.C.

She was originally invited for her involvement in the qualified opportunity zone initiative in Coatesville, PA. The situation was created by the Act Seventeen Tax Act, allowing certain distressed areas to be labeled, incentive for investors to receive tax benefits. The intention is to help the whole community at large. While Susan was visiting the White House, she talked to the press about her business, qualified opportunity zone, real estate project, and met some community minded great leaders.

Susan mentions a person makes a living by what they get, you make a life by what you give. She was very excited to be interviewed be me.

Alyssa Schriver is an alumnus of Penn Manor High School and Penn State University. She played varsity sports, and served as a team captain for the field hockey, basketball, softball, and track teams. Being the team captain allowed me to embrace, encourage, motivate and bring everyone's experiences out. She made sure everyone stayed focused before, during, and after the field hockey games. The teammates understand their roles and make the proper adjustments towards games.

I noticed her hard work truly paid off towards success for the field hockey team. They went undefeated winning the Lancaster-Lebanon League, District three, and PIAA championships. The team was driven to win every game. As a diverse team, each teammate contributed for the team's best interest, and the parents did a lot of the behind the scenes work with the booster club.

While playing Girls Varsity Basketball, she was named to the Lancaster-Lebanon League All Star Basketball team, All State, and scored one-thousand points. Alyssa enjoyed being celebrated by her family members, friends, teammates, and coaches for her proud achievement. Her name is on the banner inside the Penn Manor High School Gym.

Alyssa has a niche for running very fast as a girl, natural leadership skills, effective communication during those teachable moments, and maintains a competitive drive. When it comes to athletics it runs in the family genes, and her parents played varsity sports.

She appreciates the genuine support of her coaches, teammates, trainers, fans, athletic department, sponsors, and family members. Alyssa is a true definition of a positive student-athlete, she was awarded the Millennium Scholarship all four years at Penn State University. She and her family decided to pay it forward to a student at Penn Manor High School, through having a scholarship named after her "Alyssa Schriver".

The purpose was to award students that were similar to her in excelling at both academics, and sports. She was very honored to give back to the next class of seniors and left a lasting legacy.

Alyssa attends college football and basketball games at Penn State University. She is very thankful for the collegiate athletes for helping her get tickets, signed jerseys, and building a strong network of people. Alyssa's advice to the students-athletes is focus on school sports first, work hard, be surrounded by the right people, and have a purpose beyond playing sports.

Jasmine "Jazzy" Miller and family are a very athletic, competitive, and educated family. Her parents are Jen Lefever and Johnny Miller both Solanco High School Alumni and Student athletes. Jen played for Cross Country and Track teams, while Johnny became the All Time Leading scorer in boys' basketball. Of course, Jasmine has an older sister McKayla Miller, a Penn Manor High School alumnus. Jasmine and McKayla have a very special and unique bond together, as they would go on to compete on the same track team. They would run the sprints and relay teams.

Jen mentions every parent makes sacrifices for their children. She goes on to say her work schedule was created around her children's games, carpool, practices, fundraiser events, and games. Jen enjoyed seeing her children being positive role models, leaders, and creating positive memories together. I remember from the interview it's important for a parent to show up and be there in the present moment.

Johnny Miller mentions his daughters were very dedicated from the time they started doing sports. He maintained balance by still making it to their games, and working third shift. As their father, Johnny was always proud of them for giving their best effort as student-athletes.

Jasmine is an alumnus of Penn Manor High School and attends West Chester University. Her proud achievements are competing in California for the Junior Olympics, and winning leagues, district three, and states for varsity field hockey. Jasmine's favorite professional athlete is American track and field runner Allyson Felix.

She enjoyed spending time with Alyssa Schriver on both varsity field hockey and track. She also mentions Nicte Machado-Aco for their time together on the Lancaster City Track Club. Alyssa and Nicte made a positive influence with Jasmine doing practices, games, and wonderful memories. Jasmine is very thankful for the support from family, friends, trainers, coaches, and sponsors.

Janet Diaz, alumnus of J.P. McCaskey High School, Lancaster City Councilman member. She's a native of the Bronx, New York. She moved to the Island of Puerto Rico, living on a farm exposed to agriculture with animals, and her parents made sure she was learning how to speak Spanish lessons to learn a second language to become bilingual. Her family moved back to Lancaster, Pa and Janet graduated from J.P. McCaskey School. Her living experience in the City of Lancaster was very eye opening, diverse, relating to people that related with her.

Janet recalls multi-cultural day to fellowship, try different food, find common interest, and build relationships. She prides herself in giving back to the community, and giving a voice to those that need resources. The support of her family was very essential to her success, fellowship at picnics, celebrating holidays together, maintaining consistent communication.

Kimberly States-Gantz, alumnus of J.P. McCaskey High School and Millersville University. She did the high jump for track. Kimberly loves fellowshipping with her twin sister Kelly. They were around each other often in the small classrooms, sometimes dressed alike, and maintained their own identity. They were alike in many ways and different as they both found out who they were on individual levels.

One of Kimberly's favorite memories was her and Kelly being tall on the same soft ball team after school at Burrowes elementary school. Together they were a great duo with natural chemistry, understanding each other's nonverbal cues, and body languages.

She enjoys being a teacher that impacts the lives of children.

Kimberly is a proud mother of her children, she pays tribute to her Late Husband Collins Gantz aka Boobie through the Spice of Life Foundation. For his many contributions in the community through coaching sports, being a mentor, a leader with a passion for making the world a better place, and serving in the military.

He treated the student-athletes like his own kids, no favoritism, and the discipline provided was coming from his heart. He and his assistants went out of their way to save the lives of the youth. because it was more than winning football or basketball games, it was about learning life skills to become transferable for experiences. The impact he had in the community reflects how they supported him and his family several times over.

Kimberly was there to support the family and help take care of the student-athletes that stayed the night with their own kids. They were making sure everybody was ready to travel on the road for football camps, basketball camps, and AAU basketball events.

Kimberly's very proud moments were being there on senior nights and the high school graduation for the children. She saw her son Kobe score one-thousand points, have a national signing day for basketball, make the all-star teams for both football, and basketball.

Kimberly represents diversity and inclusion in the classroom for the students in the School District of Lancaster and society. Majored in elementary education with a focus on early childhood dual-certification. At the age of ten years old she found her purpose to become a teacher. While on the Millersville's University campus she enjoyed learning more knowledge, she completed her student teaching at Wickersham elementary school for college credits.

On Kimberly's college journey she worked very hard through taking notes, studying late nights, waking up early mornings for exams, and commuting round trip. She was very grateful for the support behind the scenes when she would come back home to relax and maintain balance in her life. The day she graduated from

Millersville University is a memory she'll always cherish and best feelings to finish.

Her work experience includes child care, learning ladder, YWCA, YMCA, and teacher for the School District of Lancaster. At Price elementary school she's known for being nurturing to the students, having her kids with her at school during staff meetings, and feeling like a family for the after-school events.

She provides inspiration to the youth that they too can become an educator, administrator, and serve in leadership positions in the education field. The fact that she's still presently teaching while overcoming her own adversities, does show the true strength, resilience, courage she has in her life. She was featured in the magazine for her many proud achievements as an educator.

Kimberly admits it was very hard to balance being herself, a wife, mother, and teacher. Collins was very supportive and demanding, as they stood together as parents, grandparents, and marriage in unity to keep going forward. The family members value being there for each other in times of need, favor, support, and aid.

I enjoyed attending the June 19th event, it represents the day African American slaves were officially free from slavery through proclamation declaration signed by Abraham Lincoln Former President of the United States of America. The symbolism of freedom was long overdue for the African Americans. Their hard-manual labor paved the way for American slave owners, bail bondsmen, Higher education industries, banks, and for-profit organizations to make billions of untaxed dollars on their backs. The slaves had no paid time off, vacation pay, sick days, personal days off, or protection from discrimination.

American Slave owners lost out on free labor as the Africans started leaving the slave plantations for a fresh start. The Great Migration moment was Africans leaving the south for the east, mid-west, and west coasts. Their desire to get away from the harsh realities of Jim Crow Laws, while adjusting to the new areas in America.

The event was hosted by the Spice of Life Foundation at Lancaster County Park. There were plenty of messages being told about African American history, t-shirts provided, games played, an abundance of food, soft beverages. The success of the event was helping the youth understand their ancestors' history. The African ancestors have sacrificed countless times, helped paved the way for future generations, and left behind a legacy that is still being remembered to this present date. The Spice of Life values families staying together, encouraging others to do better, having pride in your community.

Judge Jodie Richardson, alumnus of J.P. McCaskey High School and Millersville University. Jodie was more than welcomed to be interviewed by me. She talks about growing up in a community and family-oriented environment. The Boys and Girls club was very impactful, instrumental, provided structure, and helped to fellowship with a diverse group of people in her life as a youth.

Now she serves on the Lancaster Boys and Girls club as a board member. Judge Jodie emphasized the importance of family values, staying in consistent communication, respecting elders, taking responsibility for mistakes, and being supportive of one another. She was encouraged to become a Judge on the south east side of Lancaster, Pa. While she was working at Millersville University, Jodie took full advantage of the free tuition benefit for employees, and found her passion for helping me.

During the college semesters Jodie managed to balance work, pursuing higher education, and being a single parent. She mentions her greatest joy was going through the struggle to get there and celebrate at the Millersville University commencement ceremony. She did set the example to show her kids, and the community for being a teen mom doesn't define you or your future if you don't allow it.

With the help of her academic advisors, and mentors she graduated from Millersville University, Jodie does pay it forward in a leadership role, giving back to the community, and giving a voice to speak up for people

---

Judge Jodie Richardson Quote ""From tragedy to triumph. Today we celebrated the 10th anniversary of Ethan Vaughn and his miraculous comeback from a devastating and tragic auto accident that left him in critical condition and sadly claimed the lives of two of his family members.

Doctors gave Ethan a 1% survival rate but God had him covered at 100%. 🙌 Look at him now, a walking living miracle. We are so proud of Ethan's perseverance and drive to push forward. Wishing him continued success. 🙏 #TheVillage Go Ethan! If you see Ethan, ask him about his story. #Hope #Faith #Grace."

My interview with Jordan Steffy talked about his journey growing up in a single parent home, overcoming adversities, becoming a great student athlete, building strong relationships with mentors and professionals.

Jordan Steffy is an alumnus of Conestoga Valley High School, Maryland University, and Columbia University. He was a great

three student-athlete competing in varsity sports. While he served as a team captain on the football, basketball, and track teams. He truly excelled as a dual-threat quarterback and safety. Jordan threw tight spirals, power, and accuracy to the tight end, wide outs, and check down to the running back. He's very thankful for Coach Novak for taking him to the college camps, giving words of encouragement, mentor, and close to becoming a father-figure.

Jordan recalls his fond memories of playing midget league and middle school football, while Coach Novak was there watching on the sidelines. During his eight-grade year after football practice, he would get a ride to see how the varsity practices at Conestoga Valley High School. That must have been an eye-opening experience to see the hard work it takes to succeed in the game of life. Jordan started varsity football and basketball as a nine grader.

Jordan and his teammates played on the hardwood floors for basketball. His teammates really played with chemistry and consistent communication. One of Jordan's friend's is Ricky Hernandez, was his go-to receiver in football and setting up the plays for basketball. He and others were able to raise money to help a classmate get brain surgery. Once Jordan scored one thousand points, he used his influence to request people to donate for every point he scored.

Jordan started the Children Deserve a Chance Foundation to help make a positive impact in the lives of students. By working with amazing people to serve on the board, private donors, sponsors, volunteers, employment, and opportunity for an internship. Helping students see what their life will become before they graduate from high school, visit college campuses, and college prep help for the S-A-T, and going through the recruitment process. Some of the students went off to college, serve in the military, attend trade school, learn about coding.

He enjoyed his National signing day and committed to the University of Maryland. Jordan remembers the first impression with Head Coach Ralph Friedgen, assistant coaches, and collegiate student-athletes, and the athletic department. One of those was James Franklin, currently Penn State Head football Coach, James certainly did make most Jordan feel welcomed on the college campus, importance of staying close to home, travel to Washington D.C. and Baltimore, Md.

Jordan found a great mentor in Ed Woods, President of TerpSys. Ed gave unconditional support for the football team, University of Maryland, and Jordan's non-profit organization. I remember Ed giving me support during my times of adversities and becoming a two-time college graduate. Ed and his wife are genuine people with hearts of gold. They remember their humble beginnings and how far they've come in their own lives.

Jordan and others participated in the extraordinary give event as an opportunity to bring people together for a common cause. The event saw different organizations raising money in a twenty-four-hour time period. The prizes were awarded in two categories for most donations and most funds raised.

Jordan saw a tangible way of supporting people in their times of need and paying it forward. Later on, the non-profit organization was rebranded to Attollo.

Jordan's humble beginnings were growing up in a single parent household with his mom. His mom Sheri was there for every game, booster club, carpooling, fundraiser event, and award ceremonies. She was definitely there for her son, while working a full-time job. Jordan had a strong support system of family members, coaches, mentors, and true friends.

Denzel Kabasele is an alumnus of Lancaster Catholic High School and Native of Congo. His Uncle helped him get him an opportunity to become an exchange student and create a better life for Denzel's future. Denzel adapted to learning the English language, meeting new people, a new environment in America, and the biggest sacrifice was leaving Africa. He's a former student athlete playing varsity basketball and joined the Attollo Prep program.

Once Denzel learned about my personal walking living miracle story, and he realized I needed to share it on his YouTube Channel. He's connected with several people in Africa and other locations around the world. I was really surprised he suggested an opportunity to share my personal adversities, and near-death experience on his platform. I agreed to do the interview and find the right location with Denzel.

I was more than ready once the interview started and Denzel took the lead. We talked about the time the Lancaster Catholic Boys, and Girls basketball teams won the District three championship, on the same day, and at the Giant Center. He was very thankful I took a picture with him, as he was very happy for the team victory, and celebrated with his team mates.

Denzel started asking questions about the near fatal car accident and how I made the remarkable comeback. I was starting to feel humbled as I recall my personal experiences of hitting rock bottom. As I was being open all over again, and my heart just felt much different as I started getting deeper in the situation. My hair was very thick as an afro, since I hadn't gotten a haircut due to Covid restrictions with Barbershops, and it was very expensive to pay for a house call with a barber.

I spoke details about being dependent very much on nurses, doctors, and medical staff for health reasons. Denzel was very amazed that I had a 99% of death vs 1% chance of life. He goes on to say, God chose to use that 1% to help me be alive, use for his glory, God needed the 1% to create the miracle, and show people that miracles happen in near death situations. The 1% is what I had left to stay alive as my life still has a purpose.

Yessenia A. Matamoros is an alumnus of J.P. McCaskey High School, Art Institute of York, Founder and Owner of TruWorks. We've been friends for a very long time with common interest in business, arts, and social media. One day she contacts me to interview me and do a photoshoot for her business. We had originally planned to do everything at Musser Park in Lancaster, Pa. She had by accident forgot to bring a certain tool for her camera equipment. We put our minds together to come up with a solution and still do everything as planned.

I had called a man from Lancaster Community Television Station Channel 66, that's where I completed my previous internships at, and he was more than willing to help us out. He allowed Yessenia and Me to borrow a tool with the promise to return it the same day, and at no charge. We were very thankful for the help as a resource, and truly grateful for his help.

We arrived back at Musser Park to find the area overcrowded with people, it interfered with our initial plans, and we decided the new location will be at Long's Park. There was plenty of space to choose from inside the big park area.

Once we decided on a certain area to do the interview and photo shoot. We started setting up the equipment, finding the right lighting, and mic checks. She was in charge of taking the lead, getting the right angles with the camera, she allowed me to be my authentic self to tell my story and narrated it.

I felt very comfortable as I started opening up my heart all over again, going into details about my childhood, why I started my own LLC business, and being an inspiration around the world.

Andre Robinson is an alumnus of J.P. McCaskey High School, Fordham University in the Bronx, New York. He graduated with a Bachelor's degree in Psychology. He's a proud father, loving husband, and former football coach. Andre enjoyed being a two-sport student-athlete playing in both football and track. While Andre was serving as a team captain, he took the time to show the ropes to his classmates towards mastering their craft, and speaking up during those teachable moments.

Andre was very thankful for being around diversity to adapt towards different heritages and multitude of cultures. The experience allowed him to understand the true meaning of a true melting pot. AFS day was a very essential event at J.P. McCaskey High School for the students to fellowship together. The students were able to understand each other's differences, languages, styles, celebrate our differences, and find common ground. He believes it does take a village and it does start at home.

By Andre experiencing AFS Day, he was able to understand how the real world really is once a person became an adult. Andre learned about different music, languages, and food. He recalls the moment of eating his first Greek Gyro. Gyro is seasoned meat with herbs, spices, veggies, and Tzatziki sauce. The Tzatziki sauce is made of salted strained yogurt or diluted yogurt, cucumbers, garlic, salt, lemon juice, and herbs.

Andre finds it very important that his experiences with a diverse group of people helped him adapt towards his transition at Fordham University. He enjoyed his time at the Rosehill Campus inside the Bronx, NY, and he adapted to the transitions. By starting in the next chapter of his life as a young adult, this allowed him to find areas of improvement, as a Collegiate-Athlete. Andre played multi sports and he learned that as student-athlete wouldn't always be the best in sports.

He prioritizes when a person is a person of leadership, they should never take it for granted, there's a certain level of humility. He believes as a leader to lead by example, install certain characteristics, hard work, and be a good team.

As a father, Andre was very thankful to coach his son's together for midget league football and the Y. He mentions that those memories are invaluable, he wasn't a trophy dad, he was more concerned about how their attitudes were, and the movements of their bodies. I recall Andre mentions there are no words to describe watching both of his sons be teammates and brothers in the sports world.

His older sons are David Martin-Robinson and Darien Ressler. Andre's sons enjoyed playing midget league football, at Hempfield High School they played both varsity football and track together. I recall they would single handedly win the jumping events by placing first and second places. As brothers they learned to embrace each other. They truly celebrated what they each brought to the table, sports, and game of life. They were a competitive dynamic duo with natural chemistry, consistent communication, and respected each other.

What makes Andre and the family very proud of their son's is, when they both had national signing days earning athletic scholarships, and playing college football. The families were usually present at the College football games cheering for them, and being very supportive after the game was over.

During Darien's senior year of high school, he primed to be the best triple jump and long jump in the Lancaster-Lebanon League and District Three. He decided on doing a sport that nobody in the family ever did, which was lacrosse. He put in the time, effort, and was very coachable to learning the game.

Darien found the courage to transition to a completely different sport that he never did before. He remembers the core values that his father taught him about trying something new, accepting new challenges, and still finding success.

David was the big man on the Hempfield High School campus. He was a start in football, basketball, and track. While Darien was a star in football and track. Once they started working together all year round, they ended up complimenting each other very often, and setting the right examples for the youth that looked up to them. He and Darien learned to celebrate one another as brothers. They have a very unique relationship as student-athletes, brothers, and are full of unity to have a true come true.

While David jumped higher in the high jump event, Darien jumped farther in the triple jump event, and they dominated the long jump event together. They contributed to the success for the best interest of the team. As people started seeing David and Darien at the football games, and track events. Their presence was noticed, and recognized in the public eye with respect.

As a Husband, Andre is very thankful for the blessing of having a faithful and trustworthy wife Erin. She's an alumnus of Manheim Township High School, Eastern University, and Millersville University. Erin was an All-American at the Collegiate level.

Andre mentions a person should focus on an individual level of being the right one to attract the right one, timing is key, and self-development. He goes on to emphasize the priority of creating a safe, loving, and nurturing home. The union of a marriage is learning to work together as a team, understanding the roles, effective communication, figuring out situations on a priority level. They have a beautiful daughter named Daisy.

Andre was very humbled by the opportunity to be interviewed by me. I was glad he said yes and I emailed him the topics ahead of time. He remembers our encounters at sporting events at both football games, and track events. We took plenty of pictures together, had great moments of laughter, and found plenty of common interests. Andre congratulated me on the things I've overcome and didn't allow it to define me. He's very proud of me for being a positive role model to the next generation of student-athletes, leaders, and giving shout outs on social media.

Andre Robinson Quote from Instagram

"Humble, thank you to you. Always a pleasure chatting with you and it was an honor to sit down with you! Keep rising and shining! You're doing incredible work and sharing positivity in the community! Thank You!"

Michal Seals, alumnus of High Point Christian Academy and basketball, moving to North Carolina, and breaking the cycle. 1,000 points scored, earned a Bachelor's Degree. He's very thankful of the relationship he had with the late Collins "Boobie" Gantz. Collins was his basketball coach and mentor providing leadership.

Michal started playing basketball at the Mix, Bright Side Church,

His aunt helped him with making the big adjustment by moving down south for North Carolina in middle school. He learned how to persevere, determination, and grow more. Michal found a safe haven in basketball to become a better player, person, and develop new relationships with new teammates, and coaches.

Michal played competitive varsity basketball in both public and private school High Point Christian. He went on to become a 1,000-point scorer and graduated from West Virginia State with a Bachelor's degree. Michal loves being a proud father for his son.

Madison DeWispelaere is an alumnus of Conestoga Valley High School. She took several Advance Placement and honors to challenge herself and earn college credits at the same time. Madison enjoyed playing varsity sports track, soccer, basketball, and lacrosse. She has a creative that truly stands out in photography, graphic design, videography, web design, and social media.

Madison had the time of her life visiting California for both personal and a college tour for the Attollo Prep organization. She visited Los Angeles, San Francisco, Santa Monica, beaches, palm trees, and walked the famous Hollywood Boulevard.

She recalls meeting Super Bowl winner Torey Smith, He shared some light on his experiences of overcoming adversities, and being a positive leader. She mentions he's down to earth, very funny, impactful, and comes from humble beginnings. Madison remembers meeting and taking pictures with Earvin "Magic" Johnson. She mentions having an incredible experience hearing him talk, being engaged with the audience, and highlighting the importance of the community working together.

The support from her family was very helpful in believing in her vision for starting a business and attending Villanova University.

Madison's father's role in leadership was serving on the Lancaster City Council.

Danielle Bland, alumnus of Hempfield High School, Emory University, and Villanova University. During her time at Hempfield High School she was a standout student-athlete, winning gold medals as a sprinter, she led by exceptional example as a team captain.

She went on to break the records for the 100-meter dash and relay with her teammates. The track team was more like family to her. Danielle mentions Sarah Helgeson was a very good teammate on both the varsity basketball and track teams and a nice training partner, sprinter, team captain, and won several medals.

Her advice to future student-athletes is have fun playing sports, take care of your academics, sports can help you further your education to earn an athletic scholarship, study things that you're most interested in. Danielle's family pushed her to achieve all of her goals in sports and the classroom.

Danielle graduated from Emory University of Atlanta, Georgia with a Bachelor's degree of Political Science, Concentration in International Politics. While on the college campus, she enjoyed being a team captain, 12-time NCAA All American, Pi Sigma Alpha Science Honors Society Vice President; Google Cloud CoSIDA Academic All-American, Student-Athlete Advisory Committee. Danielle gives thanks to Hempfield High School, the awesome coaches, trainers, and teammates at Emory University, the stable support system.

The transition has been very important to show education has been very vital in her life. She's very committed to making her family proud as they support her every step of the way. Internship as a

Legal Intern at USATF for the U.S Olympic Team Trials Track and Field.

At Villanova University Danielle furthered her education for law school, she was very excited to be accepted into the program, Villanova University is one of the top ranked colleges for sports law. Fast forward to her graduation, she was awarded the Reverend Joseph Ullman award, for attaining the highest grades in criminal law and criminal procedures. Her degree is study of Sports concentration society negotiation team member.

Ricky Hernandez is a proud alumnus of Conestoga Valley High School, West Chester University earning a bachelor's degree, St. Joseph University earning a master's degree. While attending high school Ricky played varsity football, basketball, and track his senior year. He's very thankful for being on very good teams, having outstanding teammates, and coaches.

He's originally from New York, his family moved to Manheim Township School district, during his 8th grade year he transferred to Conestoga Valley School District. He made an immediate connection with Jordan Steffy, they developed a natural bond together in high school and their families fellowship together.

Ricky is a first-generation college graduate in his family, both of his parents have been married for over 20 years, they showed hard work does pay off, and provided great examples to Ricky and his sister. He feels blessed that his parents showed unconditional love, support, sacrifices, and showed up to the games. They feed his dreams to become a college coach, as he moved about three hours away from home.

Ricky made the transition from college student-athlete to coaching, he felt inspired during his senior year of college once Barack

Obama became the first black President in the USA. Doug Craft helped Ricky get his foot in the door, connected him to Coach Jeff Wilson for Ricky to become a volunteer, the next role for Ricky was once he became a grad assistant, which led to being the assistant coach at Moravian college. He accepted an assistant coach position at John Hopkins university.

Ricky is very grateful and fortunate for having a career as a college coach, a family, and a loving wife. His wife is a superhero as a Principle and raising their child.

Shavon Scott is a proud alumnus of Coatesville Area Senior High School and West Chester University. She earned a bachelor's degree, master degree, and level 2 teacher's certification. She's making a great impact in the lives of children at an elementary school. Shavon attended plays, musical events, visited radio city hall, theater. She enjoys being a loving Aunt with her nephews and nieces.

Diante Cherry, alumnus of J.P. McCaskey High School and Delaware University. He earned a bachelor's degree in sociology. He's the only student-athlete in McCaskey High School history to earn over 1,000 yards receiving and score over 1,000 points. That's a very rare achievement for any student-athlete, since most basketball players don't want to risk a serious injury from football. Diante was determined to make a name for himself, leave a lasting impression, and create a memorable legacy.

Education was key towards his success, making his family very proud, and setting the right example for future student-athletes. He was taking college level classes such as honors and AP classes. His parents were fully committed to the marathon in both high school, college, national signing day, and the graduation ceremonies. He was supported by his parents, family, friends, and he learned from his uncles.

Diante played four years of varsity football, basketball, and one year of track his senior year. He's very thankful of his teammates and coaches for making an impact and contributing. Diante was a duo with Aaron Swinton Jr, in football together, and while playing basketball they evolved into a trio with Devonne Pinkard.

Kraig Golden is a recent graduate from Howard University an Historic Black College in the Washington D.C. area. He earned a bachelor's degree in Political Science and Government. His mom worked as a college counselor and his dad is a doctor practicing medicine. Kraig set a good example for his younger siblings and led by his actions. His favorite college professor is Dr. Keneshia Grant, she's an amazing woman, teaches state, and local government. Kraig's a native of Orange County California, played high school varsity basketball. He's very consistent with his health and being in the weight room.

Joseph Wysock, alumnus of J.P. McCaskey High School, Thaddeus Stevens College of Technology, Penn College of Technology, and Lebanon Valley College with high grades in Cum Laude & Summa Cum Laude.

While attending McCaskey High School he played varsity football and basketball. He went on to Steven's Tech for Carpentry, Pennsylvania College of Technology for construction management and Lebanon Valley College for Masters in Business Administration. Joseph Wysock is a proud Husband and Father.

Aj McCloud, alumnus of Manheim Township High School and Millersville University. He played 3 years of varsity football and basketball as the center. His proud achievement was raising over 30,000 dollars from small businesses for students to have free or reduced lunch, participate in senior prom, and mini-thon.

He earned a bachelor's degree in Multiply studies Human resources and education concentration sports business.

Mental health was key towards his success and having a consistent support system. Aj attended counseling sessions, a chiropractor for his back, and he took the initiative to contact people such as family members, football coaches, learning support teachers, and friends He is very thankful of the support for crossing the finish line.

Jaime Arroyo, proud alumnus of J.P. McCaskey High School, Millersville University, and Drexel University. making his family and friends very proud. He won a Fulton Bank diversity scholarship award for college during his senior year of high school and led to working at the bank.

He earned a B.S in Business Administration at Millersville University, Jaime earned a M.B.A at Drexel University with a concentration in Entrepreneurship and Innovation Management. I remember he would take the Amtrak Train round trip to Philadelphia, Pa and back home, while working full time. The process was very rewarding for him and allowed for more leadership opportunities in his life. He's the first person in his family to attend and graduate from college. He serves on Lancaster City Council and the new CEO of Assets.

In his free time, he's active in cross fit, it involves lifting heavy weights, staying competitive, builds discipline, and maintaining great physical health. Jaime grew up as a Baltimore Ravens fan, had a great honor to meet two-time super bowl winner Ray Lewis. Jaime did volunteer at two non-profit organizations to make a positive difference in the community. Jaime is a very loving and faithful husband and father.

Michael Peirce, alumnus of Northeast High School of Philadelphia, Pa. He earned a bachelor's degree and level 1 teacher certification at Holy Family University, a level 2 teacher certification at University of Phoenix, and University of Pennsylvania. He moved to South Florida to teach for 6 years in the public school. The transition happened once he was hired by the School District of Lancaster as teaching, head girls' basketball coach, and Athletic Director at Lincoln Middle School.

Michael hired me to work the scoreboard and security for basketball games, scoreboard for football games, and freshmen track to measure the long jumps. Around the time he hired me, it helped me with my transition with getting back on my feet and becoming a protective member of society. While I was working for the School District of Lancaster after school programs, I was attending college at both Harrisburg Area Community College and Millersville University. I would attend the classes, meet with college professors during office hours, stay on top of my financial aid, and get my work done while on the campus. Afterwards, I would go straight to work at sporting events.

Michael Peirce and his assistant coaches would build great relationships with the student-athletes, parents, and teach life skills through the game of basketball.

He's very thankful of his supportive wife Jacqueline taking care of the home, while he was away coaching basketball and being the athletic director. Prior to Jacqueline meeting Michael, she did have two kids that are now adults and they have a blended family. Michael is a proud step-dad and father treated her children like his own.

He and Jaqueline have two sons together, Michael Peirce Jr. and Matt Peirce. As a father he cherished seeing his sons playing sports, taking their education seriously, and making time to celebrate their success. Michael and Jacqueline are awesome grandparents to several grandchildren.

Jade Grove, alumnus of Lancaster Country Day School and American University. I had requested her to interview me for my internship as an inspirational story. The roles had been switched around to me being interviewed and Jade taking the leadership role.

The opening started with Jordan Steffy talking about having a front row seat on my road to recovery. Jordan and his family rushed directly to Lancaster General Hospital, he mentions his heart was dropping and crushed once the sad news was true. Jordan's other family members mention being present at the hospital as they spoke with the chaplain for anything could happen, it was still a miracle that I was fighting to stay alive, the medical staff originally thought I had died on arrival.

They would be inside the visitor's room wanting updates on my health. They prayed for everyone involved in the car accident. Their prayer was answered as the Doctor and medical staff announced me as a walking living miracle. They noticed I was getting some of my personality, sense of humor, and joy back. Jordan acknowledges me as a symbol of being resilient, giving people hope, making a great difference on earth, turning a traumatic event into positive energy and fuel to make the comeback story of a lifetime.

Once Jade started to interview me that's when I knew it was time for me to be open and vulnerable about my life. I mentioned I'm a middle child for both of my biological parents for being their second child, the transition of moving to a new school district, and other things. It was my 8th year anniversary as a walking living miracle in 2019. Every year became very different as I felt depressed, down and out for each anniversary, until I experienced a breakthrough of calmness, relief, and stress free.

I can say it took some time for me to adapt to something deep down inside myself, that it did happen, and finding ways to keep moving forward. My mindset changed as I started looking at funerals as a celebration of life, the memories that have been created, and the lives that have been truly touched. Jade mentions I had my hands all over Lancaster and around the world. She asks me for advice, I give to other people that want to be involved in their community and do the same as me.

Block quote I said during the interview "

You have to find your gift and your purpose in life, because once you find both purpose and gift, you'll find out what you're supposed to do not to do, your gift will become more natural and more a blessing to other people. It's not always about getting something in return, invest in your time wisely, and making the transition looking at the long-term future of out growing people, cutting people off from holding your back."

I have found the key is maintaining balance to live your life, give back to the community, and don't allow anybody to hold you back.

I really wanted my life back together, in turn my athletic talent, poetry, and spoken word came back.

Kenny Myers, COO of Kegel's Produce recalls being a former student -athlete at J.P. McCaskey High School played football on the offensive line blocking for running back Damian Henry. He didn't mind doing the dirty work for the team's best interest. He enjoyed Senior night as he was walking on the football field with his parents there to support him. The football team he played on, was inducted in the J.P. McCaskey Hall of Fame. Some of his teammates were John Walk, Pete Horn, Tony Springer, Eric Jones, Ray Kreider, and many more.

Kenny spoke about learning the family business at Kegel's Produce with hands-on experience and working his way up to CEO. The founders were the late Earl Kegel and Mrs. Kegel, Kenny's dad, went into the business to take over from his late mother, now Kenny and his mom are in charge of the family business. Kenny's dad is remembered from being a hard worker, provider for the family, and supportive at the football games.

He mentions the family business started on Mulberry St. in downtown Lancaster city, Pa, the business evolved to a bigger location in East Hempfield Township, Pa, the clients are Franklin and Marshall College, Lancaster General Hospital, Red Lobster, and other reputable businesses. Kegel's produce gave away fresh produce to people in need and the elderly during the COVID-19 Pandemic. One of the losses was during the romaine lettuce recall, the company had to throw away 3,000 cases of romaine lettuce, there was no refund given, and it had a tremendous effect on the company. The health and safety protocols are mandated to follow in the food industry, look out for the best interest of the consumers, obeying the state and federal laws as well.

They are involved with giving back to the community and events to make the world a better place. Kenny is very thankful for the employee's that contribute to the 7-day a week operation such as; the drivers, human resources, food packers, food handlers, maintenance, marketing team, managers, chefs, accountants, and his assistant Dawn Monka. He's a firm believer of getting everything done before the day starts, with an emphasis on the produce being absolutely fresh, freshness, great quality, and very good appearance. Kenny's a proud father of three boys Kj, Kerek, and Koby.

Mr. Matt Ortega, Mrs. Corrie Ortega, and the family. I enjoyed interviewing the Ortega family at their home, very thankful to finish up my internship in Coatesville, and to go out on a high note with people I normally see often. I remember the drive like it was yesterday, once I parked my car close to their home, and rang the doorbell. The Ortega family welcomes me in with open arms, shows me the room to use, and I gave Coaches Matt and Corrie Ortega thank you cards.

As parents they didn't feel like they were making sacrifices, they were designed to do so for the best interest of the family, student-athletes, and community of Coatesville. Corrie suggests enjoy the seasons you have with your children, watch them compete, let them gain experience of trials and tribulations, and trust the process of the coaches as they are leading. Also, to be involved with the parents, kids, and other leaders to build relationships.

We completed the interview in number order with Matt aka Buggy, Tommy, Ricky, Corrie, and Matt Sr. The interview was naturally flowing, consistent, and coming from the heart. There were special moments for everybody to shine as a family united and on an individual level.

I couldn't wait to start editing the interview once I arrived at Lancaster Community Television Station Channel 66. Once I was finally done taking my precious time making sure everything was done right and fully critiqued. The footage was uploaded and ready to make its debut on television.

I even made sure the interview was published on my YouTube Channel, that way I can share the link with several people. The responses for the Ortega family interview were very positive, welcoming, and proud. The Ortega family, their friends, family, and dear loved one's truly appreciated how the interview was properly structured, conducted, and the topics relating to everyday people.

Corrie is a loving mother, faithful wife, aunt, enjoys being behind the scenes, and does plenty of workouts. She is very proud to be present for her three sons, nieces, and nephews relating to sporting events, fundraising, family time, and eating together.

Corries treats the student-athletes like her own with respect, words of encouragement, and teachable moments. She was a collegiate student-athlete at Saint Francis University running cross country and track. She's very proud to have graduated from college as the first person in her family, with a Bachelor's degree major human resources minor business management. Her job usually encourages the employees to bring your child to work day, she enjoyed having her son Buggy at Greater Brandywine YMCA for years in a row, he participated in the work exercise.

Corrie is a certified nutritionist coach helping her clients and student-athletes learn more about health, set goals, and maintain wisdom for taking care of mental health. She was truly ingrained in making sure to make a great impact in their lives and being a service to others. Corrie coaches varsity track with her co-workers, together they help contribute towards making the student-athletes at Coatesville Senior High School better, and make sure they have a plan outside of playing sports.

She and Matt were on the same track team as teammates first, they started dating, got married, and started a family together,

Coach Matt Ortega is an alumnus of Central Dauphin Saint Francis University earned a bachelor's degree and Master's degree from Millersville University. Coaching as a defensive coordinator at J.P. McCaskey High School, Harrisburg High School, York High School, and Current Head Football Coach Coatesville Area Senior High School. At Coatesville Senior High School, he earned over 100 wins, winning several Ches-Mont Championships, District 1 Championships, Coach of the Year Honors.

He's very thankful of every single one of his assistants for their contributions and the behind the scenes work. Coach Ortega goes on to thank his family, Wife Corrie, athletic department, trainers, boast club members, donors, sponsors, student-athletes, and the community of Coatesville, Pa.

He originally grew up in Steelton, Pa, his life became a transition point when he moved in with his Grandparents, and transferred to Central Dauphin High School. Playing varsity football as the starting quarterback and track teams. Matt earned an athletic scholarship at Saint Francis University to play quarterback and throw the javelin. Matt had a great experience on the college campus and graduated.

One day he contacts Scott Feldman for a coaching opportunity, Matt gets hired as the Defensive coordinator and teacher at J.P. McCaskey High School. He was learning everything under the guidance of Scott to become a future head football coach, and he was teaching Dr. Todd Mealy to be the next Defensive Coordinator. Once Matt was coaching at Harrisburg High School as a defensive coordinator and doing professional development.

An opportunity opened up to become hired as the Head Football Coach of York High School. Matt and his assistants helped rebuild the program to winning games, having the kids overcome adversities, and further their education on athletic scholarships. Pretty soon Coach Ortega was offered to become the Head Football Coach at Coatesville Area Senior High School. After much prayer with his family, he accepted the position. Matt says that any success for a head coach starts with the assistants that can become a resource.

Moving forward, he had an awesome experience coaching his sons in football, treating them like the other student-athletes, maintaining a balance between being a parent and coach. Matt does mention he was offered an opportunity to coach football on the college level, but he declined it to be there for his sons.

Family values of being a present father was the priority and that became one of the best decisions he made for the best interest of the family. By staying in Coatesville, he was able to coach his son Ricky as a quarterback 4 years of varsity, Tommy as a Wide receiver defensive back, holder, and long snapper.

Being a Head Football Coach is a blessing to mentor and be like a father figure, tough love with discipline, going through the motions of victories, losses, and earned respect.

His proud moments were being present for his older sons Tommy and Ricky's national signing day. He had been there to support several student-athletes prior to his sons playing sports. This special feeling was much different as he saw his boys become men.

He looks forward to seeing his youngest son Matt Jr. aka Buggy have his national signing day in the near future.

Matt and Corrie have enjoyed those special moments of watching their sons playing sports with their friends. They've kept building strong relationships with community leaders, parents, and sponsors, donors, and other organizations. By making sure some student-athletes that may not have both parents in the same household, can be around a positive person to provide leadership, and give a helping hand. The doors are always open, the student-athletes become family, the journey never stops once a student-athlete graduates from high school, and college.

Tommy Ortega played Varsity football playing Wide Receiver and Lacrosse at Coatesville Area Senior High School. He enjoyed having the natural chemistry with friend and Quarterback Harrison Susi for the Touchdown passes. Tommy has declared for Lindenwood University in Missouri on an athletic scholarship.

Matt "Buggy" Ortega as a student-athlete competes in basketball, Lacrosse, and football. He enjoyed being the ball boy at the varsity football games. He looks forward to playing varsity football and Lacrosse. He's very thankful for the genuine support of his friends, family, and coaches for his success as a student-athlete.

Ricky Ortega enjoyed playing sports at Coatesville Midget League "CKR aka Coatesville Kid Raiders", South Brandywine middle school, he competed in basketball, football, and track. Once he received his 8th grade promotion, it was his time to earn the starting position at Quarterback at Coatesville Area Senior High School.

Ricky's very thankful for having a national signing day, furthering his education at Villanova University on an athletic scholarship.

He likes the high academic standards, being within driving distance away from home, and still makes time to visit family.

His proud achievements are selected for the Big 33, 1st team All-State in Pennsylvania, helped lead the varsity football team to winning multiple Ches-Mont Championships, 2x District 1 Championships, winning the Javelin, He's the only varsity quarterback in Pennsylvania state football history to throw for over 2,000 yards in all four years of varsity.

He gives thanks to Jim Cantafia for being the Offensive Coordinator, mentor, and Quarterback Coach. Ricky grew up attending the quarterback camps at the Spooky Nook hosted by Jim and his assistants. Jim's previous experience of coaching was at Conestoga Valley High School, Wilson High School, Cedar Cliff High School, and Lancaster Catholic High School.

Ricky mentions the offensive line for consistent pass blocking, run blocking, pulling, and making audibles based on what the defense gave them. He humbly says without his offensive line he wouldn't have the success without them. They helped make sure his transition as a freshman was uplifting and encouraging.

Ricky was very thankful of the talented wide receivers for catching the passes, running backs for controlling the tempo of the game, tight ends for doing anything for the best interest of the team, and everybody behind the scenes as well.

Ricky Santiago was the starting left tackle as a blindside blocker for Ricky Ortega. The other offensive line were playing a vital role in making sure to outwork the defense, pick up the blitzing linebacker or safety, and make sure Ricky had plenty of time to throw from inside or outside the pocket. The Offensive lineman were coached by Steve Brazzle, alumnus of Coatesville Area Senior High School and Florida A & M.

Ricky Ortega and the wide receivers were looking for the best mismatches on the defensive backs. I noticed at the football games the defensive had to either give up the running yards or passing yards. The opposing teams were usually blown out by the mercy rule, resulting in the varsity players being pulled out to allow the other teammates to earn game experience. The wide receivers were so good that anybody could have a big game by earning yards after the catch, picking up first downs, or making the play for touchdowns. While the tight ends did a little bit of everything being asked of them. Coached by Darly Daniels,

The explosiveness of Aaron Young contributed to running, blocking, catching, throwing, and tackling. Aaron was playing in all three phases of the games such as; offense as a hybrid running back and wide out, defense a safety, corner, or linebacker, and return man on special teams. Coached by Damien Henry.

Ricky is very grateful for his teammates for making him a better football player, leader, and communication. His teammates were a very talented and special group of student-athletes that contributed towards the team's success. They provided a positive light in the Coatesville area and City of Coatesville community. Ricky and the teammates were going in the classrooms to be a positive role model and help the youth with their education. The upperclassmen took the time to share their workouts and knowledge to the younger student-athletes. Their purpose was to pay it forward, help maintain the winning culture, consistency for understanding the legacy, and upholding the traditions.

The parents, guardians, booster club members, fundraisers, events, donors, and sponsors, athletic department contribute to the success of several sports teams and the student body as a whole. That truly shows the grit and pride in the community and village. Since people keep coming together for the best interest of the kids. I believe it starts with having a common interest, building interest, and having honest conversations.

The Class of 2020 were able to have their yearbook made by Kayla Bock and other students. They were thankful for having a drive through graduation ceremony in Caln Township at Rainbow Elementary.

Kaylie aka Kalinda Vazquez and Dacia Perez are proud alumni of Lancaster Catholic High School. I had the great privilege of interviewing both of them, during their senior year of high school, and I'm very thankful they said yes.

I normally saw them at sporting events, one day in the Giant Center. It just so happened that both the Boys and Girls basketball team won the district championships the same day. I still remember that day of witnessing history being made on the basketball court. That's really rare for both a boys and girls' team to win a championship back-to-back, at the same location, and consecutively. One of them had asked me to take pictures for them with their cell phones, which pretty much opened the door for more communication, and connecting on social media.

They remember it being an amazing feeling contributing for the success of both teams, as they basketball players were awarded their gold medals, and being thankful to everyone that drove to the Giant Center. The game was tied up in the 4th quarter, it was coming down to the final seconds of the game, as David hit the game winning shot. For the girls' basketball team, they pretty much dominated the game from start, middle, and end, by playing as a team with consistent chemistry, and unity.

Kaylie took honors Spanish four, and dual enrollment classes at HACC to save money while earning college credits. She participated in being the team captain for varsity cheerleading for football and basketball. Senior night was a true for creating a positive memory at the homecoming court during half time at Lancaster Catholic High School football stadium.

They cherished visiting the Baltimore Aquarium and going out for dinner together. She gave back by being involved hands on for the mini-thon to help raise money, serving on the hospitality committee. The mini-thon event is a non-profit annual fundraiser consisting of a 12-hour long event, it does sometimes involve the four diamonds program coordinated by students in Pennsylvania, with a purpose to fight childhood cancer.

Dacia mentions a few teachers pushed her to keep thriving, work harder for what she wants to be in life, and encouragement. She truly appreciated her grandparent and mom for supporting her during senior night, won the homecoming queen crown, she enjoyed the Sweet 16 celebration for becoming a woman.

Dacia furthering her education at Millersville University and Kaylie decided to further her education at Penn State University.

Dominique Miller-Shell is a proud alumnus of J.P. McCaskey High School, father, and husband. While he attended high school, he served as a team captain for the varsity football team, contributed to the volleyball team, track team, and President of the Black Student Union.

He was grateful for playing with his teammates such as Diante Cherry, Aaron Swinton Jr. and many others. Dominique made the transition towards coaching football with the help of his mentor, while working at Lincoln Middle School he helped the students learn about media studies, podcasts, and mentorship after school program. He took it a step further by starting the Tru2You organization.

He does spoken word to express stories, emotions, and create avenues for people to embrace their creativity. The purpose is aimed towards inspiring the next generation of creatives and critical thinkers. He did contribute some writing towards a book called "Stay Alive" about suicide prevention, improvement of mental health, and having a strong support system all year round.

Dominique enjoys having a space to speak your story, tell the narrative, be yourself, without the use of going through corporate America, while he does mention my second cousin Evita Colon brand "Speak2mySoul". He believes in having an outlet, amplified, hearing the disenfranchised voices, and having our own voices.

Dominique actually contacted me to interview him, it just so happened around that time, I had finished interviewing his sister Madison DeWispelaere, and we made arrangements to conduct the interview at Lincoln Middle School. His proudest accomplishment is maintaining balance of work, pursuing his ambition, being a father, and fully supported by his wife at home.

Dr. Johnny Vega is an alumnus of J.P. McCaskey High School, Homecoming King, and native of the Bronx, NY.

Dr. Vega is very proud of me for overcoming my hardships, graduating from college twice, and being there in a time of need. He appreciated the thank you card I gave him and read the written words inside. The title said, "Blessed are the Givers", on the inside it says, "Keep living your life as you create your legacy, the teachable moments are life lessons, you have made your family proud of you, grateful are the receivers thanks so much."

His mom decided to move the family from New York to Lancaster, Pa, due to the gun violence, drugs, and gangs. His late grandfather had opened up one of the very first Spanish restaurants in Lancaster. The family moved around several times in the city, switching to different schools, and made a lot of friends. He grew up without his biological father for most of his life.

During Dr. Vega's teenage years, he started smoking weed and selling drugs to support his habit. By the time he was 18 he was selling every drug you could name and was in possession of guns, he was living a double life of playing sports, had earned a scholarship to Millersville University, and gradually moved up in the drug business. By the time he was 20 years old, started a business such as a nightclub, then his life came crashing down hill. One day in the middle of the night his club was raided by Federal agents knocking down the doors, he managed to escape, and was on the run from the law for 6 months.

He eventually got busted while driving on the road, his life was forever changed, once he spent 11 months in York County Prison. His lawyer said if there were no charges filed after 12 months the law has to let him go. One day a letter in the mail arrives, as it is opened the key words were "The United States Government vs Johnny Vega." His lawyer said if Dr. Vega gave everybody up, he would be set free with no charges as long as he testified and gave valuable information, and full cooperation, Dr. Vega refused to do that.

The second choice was a trial yet Feds have a 98.7 % conviction rate, he was facing 25 years in federal prison. The third choice was to serve 9 years with good behavior since there were no sentence guidelines. Once his lawyer gave him time alone to think about his choices, he started crying like a boy realizing his bad choices had finally caught out with him and it was a long time coming. No more going out to eat, visit his family, his business got shut down, and he started praying to God.

Dr. Vega decided to serve 9 years in federal prison, miss out on living his 20's, he was released on parole at 30 and started working at Kentucky Fried Chicken for minimum wage. While incarcerated he was very humbled for always telling the guards his number not his name, the quality of food was not good, wearing the same clothing as everyone else, and barely making any money for commissary. Once he was released from parole it was a fresh start towards being free again. He went on to turn his life around by telling the youth to be careful of who you surround yourself with.

Dr. Vega started working with the non-profit organizations to make a bigger impact in the community, redeem himself, and inspire the youth to not make the same mistakes he made. He's a proud father of his daughter Sofia.

Rosa Marti owner of Rosa's Jar, serving great quality cakes, desserts, and cupcakes. She graduated from Pennsylvania of culinary arts, local business owner, and uses her creative vision to create an appetizing appeal with food. Rosa maintained balance between work, her business, and single mother. The name of her business is very near and dear to her. Rosa is her own name, while the word jar is an abbreviated for her children's name such as Joshua, Ashlynn, Remaneata, her daughter created the logo.

What inspires her to keep going is, "When things get tough, remember why you started." That has become her why to be successful, feel people, and have them smile. Her business was thriving during the pandemic, since people had to eat, and her loyal customers supported Rosa's Jar.

Nate Phil is a proud alumnus of Lancaster Mennonite High School and Central Penn College. He played varsity boys basketball, co-ed track and field in high school. Nate played collegiate soccer and men's basketball.

Nate enjoyed his education experience to receive help, make friends, and play sports. His teammate Julian Collazo encouraged Nate to keep working out, maintain good grades, and stay strong. After not making the basketball team at Cairn University and working in a factory. Nate realized he needed to do more for his life and get back into college. At Central Penn College, he was offered an opportunity to try out for the men's basketball team and further his education. Nate made his family, friends, coaches very proud once he graduated from college.

Tracy Madhoo is a native of Trinidad, Owner of Fit Chic. She grew up in Tableland, Victoria, Trinidad, and Tobago

Her biggest transition was leaving her family and environment for America. She mentions in Trinidad, there's a melting pot of diversity and multicultural society, the food is always fresh, learning how to adapt to the industrial industry, people visiting for vacation, and Tobago has the pretty beaches. As a child she envisioned living in the U.S.A, her dream became true once she arrived, and Tracy started living the dream.

She found her niche for fixing tablets, hardware, cell phones, laptops, electronics devices. She started her business at Park City Mall in Lancaster, Pa. Then she relocated to Lancaster City. Her business was always in demand even during the pandemic, her customers were working from home, and needed their electronics fixed right away. She wanted to work for herself, be self-sufficient, create jobs, and make a great impact in people's lives.

Ethan Poetic Inspires Coach Beulah Osueke Class 3A Coach of the year at West Catholic Prep High School. She was the first ever black female coach to win a Philadelphia Catholic League Championship & PIAA state basketball championship at West Catholic Prep High School. The student Athletes and parents trusted her, providing guidance both on and off the court. Beulah leadership is full of integrity, equality, and accountability. She truly loves her players and is always a phone call, text, or email away. Beulah Osueke is a proud alumnus of Ouachita Baptist University and La Salle College.

Ethan Poetic Inspires #35 Sunshine McCrae Trinity High School Student Athlete. She and her teammates led the Trinity High School Varsity girls' basketball team. Towards winning both the 2018 and 2019 District 3 Championships at The Giant Center. Sunshine McCrae scored over 1,000 points and earned over 1,000 rebounds. She was a Mid-Penn All Star Selection and McDonald's All-American Nomination. She was playing AAU basketball for the York Lady Raiders and Maryland Belles. They are united together like a respectful family. Sunshine helped raise money for younger children to fight cancer. She attended the Homecoming Dance and Prom.

Sunshine McCrae earned a full ride scholarship, furthering her education at the University of North Carolina Wilmington. She will be going for a Bachelor's degree and will play Collegiate basketball. She later transferred to Morgan State University, a Historic Black College. Sunshine is a team player willing to do what it takes for a team victory. She communicates with her teammates both on and off the court.

Sunshine McCrae truly appreciates the genuine support of her teammates, athletic director, trainers, family, coaches, and true loved ones. Sunshine McCrae Trinity High School Class Of 2019. P.S. Thanks very much for allowing me into your life. Looking forward to seeing you play Collegiate Basketball.

My Cousin Evita Colon is the Founder and CEO of Speak2MySoul. She has written, produced, and directed her own plays. She has met Lauren Hill, Spike Lee, and many other well-known people. Evita Colon is a proud alumnus of J.P. McCaskey High School, and she earned a bachelor's degree from Shippensburg University. She played a small role in the movie with Oprah Winfrey.

Evita and I attended the same high school together. She loves being a mother to her son DJ. I like to thank Evita for giving me the opportunity to speak spoken word at her events and playing a small role in her music video.

Steve Brazzle graduated from Florida A&M University on a Football scholarship. With a Bachelor's degree in Criminal Justice. Steve is a faithful and inspiring Husband, Father, Mentor, and Coach.

Steve and I played on the same football teams together. In our 6th grade on the Coatesville Midget League and in 8th grade, we were part of the Undefeated Coatesville City Champions at Gordon Middle School. He is a graduate of Coatesville Senior High School. Steve played varsity football, basketball, Track and field. Steve was a 3-time Chest-Mont and All-Area first team selection.

His pass and run blocking skills helped paved the way for CJ Gray, Cardoza Jacks, Jeff Cellucci, Keylor, Bruno Iozzo.

Steve played alongside Georgia Tech alumnus and former NFL player Derrick Morgan. He was Coached by Tom Nichols and the assistant coaches. Thanks very much for Steve for your positive impact in the City of Coatesville community and mentoring today's students-athletes.

Kayla Bock Coatesville Area Senior High School Student-Athlete and Alumni. Kayla Bock attends Rutgers University to major in Sports Management, Masters in Administration to become an Athlete Director, and play Women's Softball. She was one of the most feared power hitters in the Chest-Mont League & District 1.

She's a four-year varsity starter in softball, swimming, and Team Captain. She's known for coming through by hitting a Grand Slam when the bases were fully loaded. Earning an invite to American International Sports Teams, 1st team All Ches Mont and All Area Honors in softball, and Winner of a Ches Mont Championship. Kayla Bock competed in swimming the 50 freestyle,100 freestyle, & 200 free relay.

Outside of sports, she enjoyed being honored on Senior night, President of the Coatesville Talaria Club for the Yearbook, & Member of the National Honor Society. Kayla truly appreciates the true love and support of her parents, family members, coaches, teammates, friends, and athletic trainers.

Roxanne Sciatta quote

"Quite an achiever she is. So proud of her and excited to see what comes in her future. She outdid herself at Coatesville and left her mark. There is no doubt she will continue to do the same throughout everywhere she goes in life. Love you the most Bop. Shine on!"

Lonnie White Jr., 3 Sport Student-Athlete star at Malvern Prep & Penn State Commit on a full Athletic Scholarship. Lonnie was playing varsity basketball, football, and baseball. He was named the team captain & a Pro Baseball prospect. Lonnie has a strong arm for throwing the baseball & football. He can jump very high to dunk the basketball and catch an Alley Hoop. For Football he made Pennsylvania 1st team All State Offense.
He made the choice to go for Pro MLB, chosen by 64th overall pick in the 2021 Major League Baseball draft by the Pittsburgh Pirates. Lonnie was fully supported by his family, friends, teammates, coaches, and others. The day of the MLB draft, his family decided to welcome people into their home, and the life changing moment happened once he was drafted. The tears of joy and loud cheers from just about everyone is truly cherished. Lonnie is committed to working out all year round and helping build up his teammates. He truly appreciates genuine love & support. Of family members, trainers, coaches, and the community.

DJ Diamond Kutz

Ethan Poetic meets the one and only "Dj Diamond Kutz"

She's one of the best female Dj's not only in the Philadelphia area but the entire U.S.A. At an early age her dad invested in her with gifts of music, guidance, and Dj equipment. As she became older, she soon started dj'ing at people's homes, sweet sixteen, radio stations, and business events. The main reason why she's one of the best female DJs in the entire U.S.A.

She practices to improve her skills on a year-round basics. From the sound mixing, turntables, music selections, and much more little details. I was honored to meet her in person and cherish this moment.

Ethan Poetic is proud of his Puerto Rican Heritage, history, and identity. The mixture of Puerto Rican is African, Taino Indian, and Spanish. The USA granted all Residents of Puerto Rico USA Citizenship. My late Grandfather Benito Rivera- Lebron & several family members left the island of Maunabo, Puerto Rico.

They were seeking better opportunities and quality of life in the USA. They sacrificed leaving their homeland and created a new life in America. They still went back to visit the Island of Puerto Rico for fellowship and family gatherings.

A new generation of family members were born and helped paved the way for more opportunities for the future generations. Starting over can be a good thing. As long as it has a greater purpose to impact the lives of others. For growth, education, and health. Knowing your history is part of your Identity.

Coatesville humble beginnings

Ethan Poetic is a proud native of Coatesville, Pa. I come from very humble beginnings. I choose to go back to where it all started from. To pay my respects, put the pride city of Coatesville on the map, & on social media. I remember where I came from such as attending Caln Elementary School & Gordon Middle School.

I used to play football at Scott field and practiced Basketball at the Legendary Ash Park. Coatesville Area School District has a wealth of talented student athletes, plenty of diversity in the community, and a rich history of success stories.

I'm one of those success stories. It's very humbling and gratifying coming back, as a Harrisburg Area Community College, and Millersville University Graduate. I usually make time in Coatesville at the football, basketball games, & visiting family members.
Once a Red Raider, always a Red Raider.

Millersville University picture

Ethan Poetic is officially a Graduate of Millersville University. With a bachelor's degree of Science minor speech communication & media.

I like to thank my college professors, academic advisor James Machado, classmates, writing tutors, and math tutors. With your help and guidance, I've crossed the finish line.

I like to thank Jordan Steffy, his lovely Wife Kiandra, & Attollo formerly known as Children Deserves A Chance Foundation. For encouraging me to pursue higher education & taking me on college tours. Being there in the moments of both high, low, and medium points in my life.

Of course, honor, glory, & high praise to God. For allowing me to be a walking living miracle. 99% of death vs 1% of life. Miracles do have every day on earth. Today my life is forever changed for the better. as I enter new Chapters of my life.

Ethan A. Poetic

Millersville University Graduate

Class of 2020

Application for graduation

Ladies & Gentlemen, I'm proud to Announce. I've submitted my application for Graduation from Millersville University. With a Bachelor's Degree of Science. Major speech communication minor broadcasting and media.

Plans to pursue a career in Television, Radio, & Motivational Speaking. This is for myself, the City of Lancaster, School District of Lancaster, The City of Coatesville, & Coatesville Area School District.
My Education Journey started in Coatesville Area School District from Pre-k until halfway of my 8th grade year. A family decision was made both moving & transferring to the School District of Lancaster. At Wheatland Middle School I received my 8th grade promotion. I ended up Graduating from JP McCaskey High School. Enclosing I will always remember where I came from, my humble beginnings started in Coatesville, Pennsylvania, born at Brandywine Hospital, & have evolved in Lancaster, Pennsylvania. Thank You for those that helped me on the journey of pursuing higher education.

As I was typing inside the PDF for my College Application for graduation, I knew it was time to have a big celebration and invite plenty of people. December 2020, the day after Christmas, I had my celebration with food, soft beverages, a video slideshow, music, and a toast with Sparkling Apple Cider. I gave a memorable speech and uploaded it to my YouTube Channel. Thankfully, I had a video person record everything and upload to my YouTube Channel then I emailed the link to anybody I knew.

While at Attollo Prep. I was in for a big surprise that really blew me away. Two staff members totally surprised me out of nowhere without the confetti and fireworks. They gave me a package, but I wasn't sure what was inside of it. I was told to open it up once I got home, Instead I chose to presently see what was inside. I realized this is a special moment to create a video and share it with social media. With the help of those two staff members of Attollo Prep, that moment is forever ingrained in my mind. I had made the Attollo Prep Dean's List and was awarded an Attollo hoodie.

For any college student, making the dean's list is such a high honor. It takes a serious commitment to have a high G.P.A.

I had a celebration for my 10th year anniversary as a walking living miracle. This time with the help of my cousin Shannon Thomas, an interior decorator. She and her helper were able to create my vision into life with a red and black color theme.

The purpose was to have a celebration of life as I overcame the life challenges and still made positive progress. Not too many people can say they overcame death and still managed to live a productive life, graduate from college twice, and be admired by the youth. After the celebration was over, I dedicated myself to let go of some balloons as a symbol of letting go of the pain I endured.

Even when I was going through the pain, I never turned to drugs on the streets or started drinking excessive amounts of alcohol to self-medicate. The pain did go away over time, not that time heals all wounds. Sometimes in life I have to keep a distance from certain people that can cause triggers or look to create drama for attention. I set my boundaries in my life, knowing how far to go or fall back.

I was featured in the Harrisburg Area Community College newsletter for being a Walking Living miracle and proud alumnus. My mentor Bob Paul contacted Dr. Theresa Russell-Loretz, the

Head of the Department of Communication and Theater. He told her about my amazing comeback story and everything I'd overcome. Dr. Russell-Loretz, Millersville University Professors, and staff members had no idea of everything I overcame as I kept pursuing higher education.

She decided to surprise me with a "Department Chair's Special Overcoming Adversity Award". Even though I wear glasses, I just didn't see that coming at all. Of course, I created a video to thank her very much for everything she helped me with as a student at Millersville University.

I was at a Chester High School Basketball Game with Dave Burman, York College Graduate and Varsity Sports Announcer. He had invited me to the playoff game and Chester High School won the game. After the medal ceremony, I received a text from John Walk of Lancaster Newspaper expressing his strong interest in doing a follow- up story for my 10th year anniversary.

John Walk & I completed the interview at Attollo Prep's office and a Professional Photographer came to my after-school sports program job at JP McCaskey High School inside the Barney Ewell Stadium. It was a very competitive track scrimmage between McCaskey vs Coatesville Area Senior High School. I have ties to both School Districts, both in a past and present way.

In the spring of 2021, with the help of Lancaster City Council Member Janet Diaz, I received a Proclamation Declaration. The vote was a Unanimous decision from all Lancaster City Council Members and Mayor Danene Sorace. I framed the legal document and cherish it with each passing day.

I was featured on Lancaster Community Television channel 66 being interviewed by Diane Dayton. Her show is called "Behind the Lines", giving an updated follow up on my ten-year university, two-time college graduate, inspiration in the community, and on social media.

We did the mic checks, adjusted the lighting, set up three cameras with the tripods for different angles, and a review of the questions she would ask me. I remember thinking she's in charge of her show and I'm a guest being featured for my inspirational story. The thought of making up a joke could mess up the flow or be funny. There just needed to be good timing with allowing that side of me to speak naturally.

I'm being vulnerable all over again this time for the greater good to inspire people around the entire world. I wasn't planning on crying at all like some people may do with being that open. Looking back on the Oprah Winfrey show her guests expressed laughter, empathy, tears of joy, compassion, closure, and much more. Each guest shared either their story or personal experience of their lives on television and it usually captures the attention of the audience.

On Diane Dayton's Show, I get to tell my story in my own words and tell the narrative. The freedom of expression did allow me to be more of myself, and turn my personal adversities into my advantage. The humility does humble the hearts of many people for seeing a true comeback story.

I talked about being presented an opportunity to do poetry at Lancaster Country Day School. Andrew Williams approached me with the idea since his teacher wanted a spoken word artist in the classroom. I was asked several questions during the interview process and tested on the spot to present poetry. The teachers and administrators were convinced of my skills.

I was ready to show my artistic side with the students, allowing them to use their imagination, and communicate in their own words. The day I went inside the classroom, a simple introduction was done for me, and it was time to deliver the arts.

As the students were seeing how I wrote on the white board, they noticed my examples, metaphors, and analogies related to them. Their interest began to grow overtime with questions, sharing their poems, and the teacher was very impressed with how the class gravitated towards me. I must have made the first impression really count with everyone.

After I left the classroom, I realized I can be a keynote speaker, do poetry workshops inside the classrooms, and start my own business.

During my interview with Diane, she mentioned that I inspire other people from all different groups and backgrounds. I mentioned it started with student athletes, local leaders, business owners, and Attollo Prep sponsors. Everything just happened naturally with inspiring people in a type of grassroot way. Nobody saw it coming or maybe the people that were praying for me saw my life's coming attraction.

Diane says I'm fearless since I overcame a lot of adversities and personal challenges in my lifetime. I used to be afraid of things when I was a child and teenager. Over time as I became older and wiser, I stopped being afraid of certain things that were already conquered by previous generations and my ancestors. Fear is just an emotion that can be a minor distraction or a stronghold that needs to be addressed on a priority level.

There's a difference between being aware of your surroundings, the people in your inner circle, false, evidence or reality appearing real. I believe there's a need to address the truth on a root level and individual levels.

I do go on to mention I grew up without my biological father, transferring from Gordon middle school to Wheatland middle school, my athletic coaches, and building relationships. Depending on the circumstances, a child or children can make it in this world without the biological father. Some people do have children unplanned or planned. While the child or children still has a purpose in life, to fellowship around positive male leaders to experience manhood, masculine energy, mannerisms, and respect.

On Thursday April 1st, 2021, my boss, Mike Patton, texted me around 5am in the morning saying I made the front page of the Lancaster Newspaper. Then a former coworker shared a screen shot from the Lancaster Newspaper and tagged me on Facebook. Before I knew it there were over 400 shares on Lancaster Online Facebook page of the featured story about me.

I thought I would need security guards for when I came back to work and went shopping at Target, Walmart, or Office Max. OK, that's a joke, but I did feel really famous for a few days. I bought over 20 newspapers to give away to certain special people in my journey so they would have copies. I framed the copies I kept for myself to cherish my legacy and memory.

May 2021, I received communication from WGAL News Anchor & Reporter Barbara Barr. She's a proud alumnus of J.P. McCaskey High School, Boston University, & American University. Barbara Barr & I did the hometown Inspirational interview at Attollo Prep's office with Jordan Steffy. Prior to the interview being conducted, I had to be at work from the early morning until 3pm or 3:30pm. Afterwards I rushed straight home to get my personal belongings for b-roll footage and take pictures. Once I arrived at Attollo Prep it was show time.

Jordan had just finished up his meeting, Barbara Barr and her cameraman were ready to get everything started. The cameraman was setting up the lighting, wireless microphones, and Barbara was looking over her notes. In the meantime, I was very happy to finally have an updated version of my inspirational story on a bigger television network. This time people can move forward to the positive things I'm achieving in my life and the impact being made.

Once the camera started recording we had a brief conversation with open ended questions, afterwards we got into the meat and potatoes of the interview. I thought I was more than ready to answer the questions and give my best responses.

Barbara and I had a blast together as the conversation was naturally flowing. I suppose since we're both J.P. McCaskey Alumni: that's where our chemistry came from. Please keep in mind everything is taking place the same day I have a Commencement Ceremony at Millersville University. After the interview was over I felt relieved that history was being made on such a special day.

I drove out of town to pick up my father figure Anh Hai as we soon arrived on Millersville University Campus. He was there to support me since he remembers me being a teenager and growing into a man with greatness. The emotion he expressed was very proud of me for everything I've overcome, perseverance from, and inspiring people around the world. Anh Hai truly did enjoy and treasure the special moment in my life as I crossed the finish line at Millersville University.

That same week, I was featured on WGAL for the Inspirational Story of my 10th year anniversary. I recorded it from my I-Phone 7, and uploaded it on my YouTube Channel. Afterwards, I sent the link to several people in emails and on my social media to share that updated special moment with people. The responses I received back were very positive and humbling. From several family members, childhood friends, teachers, college professors, and much more.

I'll always remember the work it took to cross many finish lines and break barriers along the way.

In July 2021, I signed a lease for a brand new 2021 Honda Civic and made a video to enjoy the special moment. Afterwards, I received in the mail a Pennsylvania Commonwealth Citation from Pa State Senator Scott Martin. He's an alumnus of Lancaster Catholic High School, Millersville University, and a Republican.

August 2021, I was awarded a second Pennsylvania Commonwealth by Pennsylvania House of Representatives Michael Sturla. He's a proud alumnus of Kansas University & Democrat. It felt great to be on the positive side of politics for the greater good, with praise coming from both sides of the aisle.

August 2021, with the help of Kegel's Produce. I was invited to throw out the first pitch at the Lancaster Barnstormer baseball game, awarded 12 tickets, free soft beverages, and sky box seating. I made sure to warm up my body and practice throwing the baseball ahead of time.

I was waiting patiently for instructions to throw out the first baseball pitch. With nearly a thousand people watching. My name was called in front of the crowd, I waved back at people, and threw the baseball over the plate, the crowd cheered very loud. I sure didn't want to end up on anybody's blooper reel! My guests and I enjoyed the baseball game, took pictures, and made it back to our homes.

Capping off this period of honors, I was invited to join the National Society of Leadership and Success, America's largest leadership honor society. Less than five percent of all students nationwide are even nominated to participate.

April 22, 2016, I attended a special event hosted by Millersville University and the guest speaker was a well-known educated woman. She's been on tv, wrote books, and does offer counseling services. I walked up to the microphone and asked to get a picture taken with her. She turned me down stating she would have to take pictures with everybody else. She offered to take a selfie with the crowd, one of the ushers had helped her to set up her cell phone and the selfie pictures were taken.

As I started walking back to my seat, an alumnus of Millersville University asked for my cell phone and told me to stand right next to the stage as she started talking again. The alumnus started taking pictures of me and the woman as she was talking center stage. Meanwhile, the crowd starts laughing very loud and hard out of control.

The woman looked down at me with the microphone in her hand saying" Now Ethan you have ruined my Etiquette." That's exactly when the crowd really lost it, I was only doing what I was told, and the pictures were saved on my cell phone. I posted the picture on my social media, one of my family members commented on the post saying" Ethan You're lucky security didn't take you down for that! lol Love you E!"

In March 2017, I was able to have a sign created for my 6th year anniversary as a walking living miracle. Thankfully, there were arrangements made to meet and take pictures with Dr. Steven Woratyla MD. He and other people on the medical team performed the high-risk emergency surgery. Nobody was even sure if I was going to make it alive. I was told one of the nurse's had tried very hard thinking I didn't make it back to life. She was hugged by many coworkers for support as the tears were dropping out of her eyes.

The following day when she returned back to work, her coworkers gave her the great news that I did make it back to life, resting peacefully on the hospital bed, with visitors in the room, and waiting inside the visitor room. She was filled with rejoice inside her heart, as she now cried tears of joy, since a miracle had taken place at Lancaster General Hospital. I don't know the names or faces that helped perform that emergency surgery. That day must have been filled with emotional highs and lows.

I remember the day I had decided not to work; the purpose was to volunteer hosted by "The Men of Iron". I enjoyed my experience of serving for a greater situation for which lives were forever changed by this organization. The event was held at the Lancaster Convention Center, I just so happen to meet and take pictures with Tony Dungy.

Tony had a security team protecting him, in fact Tony initiated a fist pump with me, that really surprised me a lot. Once he came back around from a brief walk through of the venue, one of his security guards asked for my cell phone to take pictures of me and Tony together. It was such a high honor and pleasure to take pictures with a super bowl winner as a player and first as an African American Coach.

He gave a great speech on the mentors that invested in him, his parents for believing in him, the support of his friends, and giving his best effort as he entered new chapters of his life.

Chapter 11. Randy M. Vaughn

My older brother is Randy M. Vaughn, Coatesville Area Senior High School alumnus. Between me and Randy there is a big age gap. I don't know about his early childhood and living with our mom as a single mom of one child. We have two different dads with the same biological mother. As I am looking back on my memories, he went from having our mom's undivided attention to receiving less and less once me and our other siblings were born.

By the time Randy graduated from Coatesville Area Senior High School he would spend a lot of time playing basketball at the legendary Ash Park, taking the time to play against his classmates, friends, and people from out of town. Randy would work on mastering his craft. He took time to support the youth playing summer league basketball at the park. I know, looking back, he was definitely athletic.

He was always better than me due to the age difference between us. We would always play video games together and he usually won. I took my humble defeats and lessons learned from Randy. The Sega Genesis was his niche, as it was inside the living room and bedroom. The funny part is things started changing as he started working and spent more time outside of the household.

I started having victories over him in the video games since the tides had turned into my favor. The PlayStation, PlayStation two, and Nintendo 64 became my niche. I guess those losses I took from Randy did not discourage me at all. He would sometimes watch over me and my siblings at home. The stepdad that was dating our mom for eight years and one day left out the door with his personal belongings packed up still maintained a relationship with us and co-parented with our mom.

Once Randy started working a job the responsibility was put on me by our mom. There used to be a babysitter for me and my siblings to watch over us. I can remember two different women watching us when we went over to their homes. One day we suddenly stopped going to the babysitters and I did not know why the responsibility was put on me. I just know it led to me missing out on my personal growth.

The family went from living in Caln Township to the City of Coatesville. We lived on 18 Oak Street, on a hill with plenty of residual housing. Several years later we ended up moving to 626 South Ave, this time without my older brother.

I just remember he had not come with the family and that it was our mom's choice. To live in the new home without my older brother felt different and surreal. I only saw Randy at family gatherings and walking around the streets of Coatesville.

I was sometimes watching my younger siblings at the new home. I still wanted to do something different besides being at home with my siblings. I saw Randy less and less once the family moved to Lancaster. Fast Forward to the summer of 2009 on a family trip to Orlando, Florida. That is the last time I saw him alive as a man standing on his two feet.

The winter of 2009, we talked on the phone leading towards our last verbal conversation. Then, in January 2010, he passed away due to gun violence. It was the first murder of the year in Coatesville, making headlines across Chester County and the United States. I went from second born to the eldest brother overnight without preparation or guidance.

The funeral, burial, and the trial were very stressful for everybody that knew Randy. I never wanted to see him go out like that as a human being. I still pay my respects to his grave site to reflect on what my life has become without him.

I have surpassed him in age as I am still alive today. Sometimes I wonder how he would feel about me being the older brother, since the torch has been passed on to me. Normally the first born is giving the rite of passages, higher regard, and more blessings for making it easier for more siblings to enter the world through labor. Randy passed away young, gone too soon, and still remembered by family and community members of Coatesville.

A panel of four men and eight women found the man guilty of first-degree murder. He is serving a life sentence. There was justice served that day inside the Chester County Courthouse. No stone unturned in the conviction of the shooter being found guilty by a jury of his own peers.

Randy's death was a heart-breaking ordeal for anybody that knew him. For him to be shot down in an alleyway and left for dead without help to stop the internal bleeding was gut-wrenching. Receiving of the phone call brought chills down my spine, heart, and mind. There is no good way to receive any type of news about a family death.

A life gone too soon leaves people simply speechless, especially when it is due to gun violence. I had taken some time to stop watching crime shows and playing shooting video games since they were associated with death or guns. It took some time adjusting to the fact that he was gone and not coming back. Things got better with time as the adjustments did happen.

Later I ended up meeting Jordan S. Steffy at that life changing In the Light Ministries Saturday service. Maybe that was my wake-up call to keep moving forward in my life as I still have a purpose to fulfill.

Chapter 12. My Path with Poetry

I learned how to write from attending public school in Coatesville Area School District and School District of Lancaster. I often read books, newspapers, the bible, newsletters, posters, flyers, and documents. What got me into poetry was noticing a transition with music. It was not as creative or original like it once was. The music business was forever changing, artists did not like the contracts, while everyone else got paid more.

In return artists started withholding their best music works for a mixtape or a future contract in their favor. I believed in my ability to write better than most artists or musicians at that time.

As a teenager, I wrote everywhere I went, whether it be at work, home, in a car, at school, on the bus, and traveling to different places.

Every year I got better and better. The flow was more natural and fluid. Keep in mind, I never intended to recite my poems or special speeches. I was just keeping everything to myself for safekeeping. I only showed a select few people the writings.

My life was forever changed once my older brother tragically passed Away. Prior to his death, I offered to speak a poem at a baby shower.

Once I spoke at the baby shower more doors opened up for me. I opened for Black Ice a.k.a. Lamar Manson at Crispus Attucks Community Center.

One day I went to the Puerto Rican Parade. I realized I needed to walk and speak at this event. I ended up connecting with Paul

Rodriguez, since he knew the board members or committee of the Puerto Rican culture center.

He remembered me from a couple of events I spoke at. Once he introduced me to the students and the committee, it just so happened I had my Puerto Rican parade poem written and ready. Paul trained me to work on my stage presence, engage with the crowd, give myself a brief pause in between important words, and speak a Spanish statement as my conclusion.

Paul was really patient with me, as he had me start over to perfect my craft and reflect on how this would be remembered at the parade. The day of the Puerto Rican Parade was really big, I walked from East Orange Street into West Orange Street into downtown Lancaster. I should have been inside a car that day instead of walking. As I was getting ready to perform, something almost went wrong. The announcer forgot to introduce me for my time slot. Luckily Paul came to the rescue to make sure I performed, and the changes were made.

Once I was introduced my nerves were on full tilt as I was finally ready to perform. I had a good beginning, an alright middle, and the close was great because of the Spanish statement. After I was done, my nerves came back to normal, and Paul was very proud of me. The best part was that Ricky Hernandez recorded the performance and I was able to upload it to my YouTube channel. I was able to share the video with anyone that was interested in seeing it.

As a young boy, I grew up watching karate movies and shows. I enjoyed seeing the action-packed movies, stunts, and acting with subtitles translated from Chinese to English. The man that stood out the most was Bruce Lee. It's funny that I saw him as such an idol that I copied his moves and read the books on karate. Many years later, I found out he had already passed away. Shocked, I thought he was still alive, only to realize it is his legacy that is still alive.

He had become an international movie icon, movie star, and had a larger than life fan base around the world. Bruce involved his time with family, marriage, and finding something new to master in life. Now when I look back on the influence he had around the world, there are plenty of stories he left for people to remember and apply in their lives. Bruce had his share of struggles and hardships in the USA, but he went on to turn those things into his advantage.

Barry Sander is a man of faith, humble composure, and consistent work ethic. I idolized him as a football player that gave his all regardless of his size. He still proved people wrong, as he went on to achieve many things both on and off the football field. He invested a lot into the game of football in high school, Oklahoma, and Detroit Lions. He is what inspired me to become a running back in midget league football. I was small in stature, quick, plenty of juke moves, and heart. I studied the game, listened to the commentators, reviewed the highlights, and played NFL Madden football.

Football and sports is my outlet, building relationships, and excitements, and became my muse. Sorry ladies, sports are my first love, safe haven, and outlet.

Deion Sanders was very instrumental in my life when I saw he had world class speed, flashy moves, and a larger-than-life personality. I meant that on the football field he took care of business, created his brand, and won super bowl rings. Once he gets off the football field he goes back to his family, mentors, and gets involved in the community.

Here are several of my poems listed.

Bible Study

God can take away your wounds, scars, trauma, and personal problems.

That's only if you're willing to go there.

You'll be so surprised by what can take place.

In only a brief moment of your time.

Praying is the direct line of communication.

Praise and Worship goes even farther.

Forgiveness, closure, bitterness, and compromise.

It's better to release and let go.

Then go about handling your own business.

So many spirits inside of us that we don't even know about.

Turn away from the detour, choose the best route.

To be set free with freedom.

Where do you go from here?

Acknowledge negative.

Be open minded to the positive.

Leading towards know the true motive.

We can be our own worst enemy.

We can learn to live more peacefully.

Maybe your faith is at a low point.

Better to create a support system.

Then it can be restored.

First you must really want it.

What I should have done when I had the chance!

Be more committed to playing varsity sports.

Such as football, wrestling, and track.

Going to practice and lifting the weights.

Be more involved with the community.

By understanding what leadership is about.

Would have been the fastest on the co-ed track team.

Spring 2003 my 10th grade year.

My height and weight measurements were 5-9 and a half, between 128 – 132 pounds.

You can say I'm light and slender.

At the same time, I'm ready to take flight.

Looking back, I could have been the team captain.

Breaking records to be published in the newspapers.

Football I played for fun.

During the 2001 summer workouts it was very hot under the sun.

Seriously, I rather run in the morning without the sun.

Wrestling was good, learning a lot of moves.

I still have my 3rd place medal.

Probably would have made districts and qualified for states.

As for now, I'm still athletic enough to keep playing sports.

Overall, do everything you can while you're still young.

Don't cover up your wounds

Give it time to heal.

So, your heart can really heal.

You're not the only one, as other people know how you feel.

What young people are going through is real.

Maybe you need to let go of the strings of attachments.

So, you can fully grow.

Life is full of highs and lows.

Are there positive solutions people can do?

So that you make it all the way through to experience a breakthrough.

Why haven't you noticed how you grew.

Before you were crying yourself to sleep.

Then tell me all of the secrets you used to keep.

What you got yourself out of or into was deep.

Now where do you go from here.

To help you put everything behind you in the rear.

Looking at yourself in the mirror.

You have every reason you cheer.

Take it from me.

You'll only get better in due time dearly.

It's your choice to take control.

Don't put yourself backtrack by taking a toll.

Don't cover up your wounds.

Or you're going to be carrying a lot of the weight.

Tuesday Church

They've changed my life with good intentions.

Maybe I can give back.

Since I became a better person.

Maybe God is using people so children and teenagers.

For better guidance and leadership roles.

Starts within the heart.

The whole mind, body, and soul.

A battle might come up.

Be wise during the struggle.

Know your surroundings and the lay of the land wisely.

So, you have complete victory.

I enjoyed the summer programs.

To remain active in life.

The mind should learn something new every day.

To keep on growing.

Leave what you've been through, leave it at the door or the cross.

Sometimes the past comes in the present time.

You can let it all go.

So, you become a better version of you.

Puerto Rican Parade

We're all making history.

Thanks to the law firm for paying the police fee.

As we gather on the street.

Remember what helped makes this event possible.

Every decision count as time passes by.

Always thank our ancestors since they come before us.

They've helped lay down the foundation and platforms.

So that we can take what's given to us.

Towards a higher level to exceed exceptions.

The history of Puerto Rico overcame its own struggle.

The culture still lives on today this present day.

Not to mention the future.

Be thankful for having freedom.

Be thoughtful for being a U.S.A Citizen.

In the meantime, enjoy the weather.

Give respect to the speakers and dancers.

They put in a lot of time and effort.

Just to be on point for this special moment.

Simply raise your flags.

Cheer loud and be very proud.

For living your life to the fullest.

As for respect.

We have to earn it by giving it.

This is where it always starts.

Amour is deeper than what we notice in our actions.

Trust is what we earn.

The Puerto Rican Parade is truly special.

Yet we remain humble and full of unity.

Cherish the moment we have now.

We'll soon look back on it.

As a distant memory.

Clyde E. Brown II

Thanks for being a great friend and father figure.

Nine years ago, was when you first saw me.

From our sense of humor's.

You're a man of Knowledge.

Giving the truth and wisdom.

Our bond grew tight overtime.

Because we both offered something different.

You're from the old school, while I'm from the new school.

Our ways of thinking will impact each other.

Eating lunch with you was the best.

Hearing your life stories and random jokes.

All the years of my high school journey at J.P. McCaskey.

You're one of my favorites of all time.

You knew more about life than most people.

Your point of views made a good influence.

My 12th grade year you saw me turn into a man.

Who has the potential to do anything in life?

Whether you're a dad, grandpa, friend, uncle, great grandpa, and co-worker.

You always believed God does great wonders.

I accepted him into my heart

For a brand-new start.

Our friendship will always stay together.

P.s here's a DVD as a gift when I got baptized.

Now here's a chance to see it with your eyes.

Spread word about my talent.

The proof is in your eyes.

To show people of all ages.

As for now, enjoy life.

This is my way of giving Thanks and returning the favor back to you Mr. Clyde E. Brown.

Friendship Letter to Ernie and Elmina Beiler

2002 was when we saw one another face to face,

The summer season in Sterling place.

With no time to waste.

I was invited to Tuesday church.

It's a place for teenagers and children.

The adults are in charge.

With open arms the youth gain bible knowledge.

The leaders invested their time, money, and resources.

Simply because they truly cared from the bottom of their hearts.

They welcomed people to their homes and farmland.

I still remember the organic garden.

So much time has gone by.

How did I manage to get this far?

Without being under the proper guidance.

No real father.

He can save the excuses don't bother.

A real man can only learn life lessons, mistakes, history, and humility.

To become a better version of a real man.

To Way of Jesus Ministries thanks for being in my life.

Because of you I accepted God by wanting the right purpose.

You have earned your college degree

College degrees are not given out.

They are earned and worked for.

By taking the time to study and research information.

During all hours of the night and early morning.

Even when you feel like sleeping by laying your head on a pillow.

There's no telling what your potential really is.

The journey is part of your purpose.

The path does have a finish line.

The everyday choices do add up.

Figure out your major right away.

Skip the delay.

Just to keep everything moving.

So many degrees to choose from such as Associates, Bachelors, Masters, and Doctorate.

Money is invested daily.

Keep in mind by staying fully committed.

College history started in Europe and evolved around the world.

Applied knowledge is power.

Education and experience get you so far in life.

Stay true to yourself.

Congratulations You have earned your college degree.

E.A. Sports NFL Madden Football

You have to be very good at all three phases of the video game.

21 blowouts put your opponent to shame.

Offense makes the first downs to move the chains and put points on the scoreboard.

Defensive stops and turnovers will put a halt to the drive.

Special teams is mostly about gaining the best field position.

Don't fall for the play action or Run pass option.

That's just a distraction.

Turbo blitz should be in your play calling.

Len Green aka Dynasty was part of Game Time Philly.

Eric Wright aka the Problem was the best on the west coast.

Strong nickel can cause stress to an offense.

Having enough protection in the offensive line for the test.

Take out the competition.

E.A. Sports bus in Time Square, New York, with four players left to declare a winner.

Samson and Microsoft are the sponsors.

Switching game systems having players adapt to different playing styles.

The controllers are PS2, Xbox, Xbox 360, and PS3.

For every game played.

For every dollar made.

The video game market growth wouldn’t stop.

Each play has its own strength and weakness.

React fast, don't be nervous.

Getting the win helps you gain confidence.

Getting better takes time.

Being one of the best takes patience.

My 23rd Birthday

Having a wonderful Birthday as I want to go to Long's Park.

I saw the ducks in the pond.

Everybody came together to form a bond.

The turtle was swimming under the water.

As we watch over looking into the water.

Being picked up takes money, time, and gas.

This will be a memory to really last.

Being around people with class is such a nice task.

Everything that took place I didn't even ask.

The birthday card was so enjoyable.

The balloons float without a care.

All of the gifts for me are wonderful.

Maybe there's more to come.

Maybe I should enjoy the moment.

I give thanks for everybody giving me compliments.

Doesn't matter how small or big the amount.

It's more than the thought that counts.

It's the action that speaks behind it.

Apple Bee's the time of my life.

Cutting the grilled chicken and steak with a knife.

Three rounds of pineapple juice.

Plus, twelve fried Honey BBQ chicken wings.

To Children Deserve a Chance Foundation deserves a toast.

I truly appreciate the Armor from those who know me closely.

Turning 23 is still youthful.

Life for Ethan A. Vaughn goes deep as can be.

Looking forward to the future, quite frankly, how far can I go with Poetry.

May I receive the answer sooner than later.

Randy M. Vaughn Tribute

To my older brother, Randy M. Vaughn

Your death is something to remember.

I haven't felt this way since my late grandmother passed away.

Everything happens for a reason and purpose.

Life is way too short.

My older brother is gone.

I can only imagine what took place.

Shot several times as he goes down on the ground.

On the ground he lies taking in deep breaths.

The neighbors call the police as the driver and passenger get away.

Sounds of the sirens arrive at the alley way location of 200 Diamond Street.

I've become the older brother overnight due to gun violence.

I'm left with power and responsibility at task.

Now to figure out what to do next as I keep moving forward with my life.

You're the older brother I wouldn't forget.

My life, role, and world has been forever changed.

Be very aware the forensics team is there with yellow tape at the crime scene.

What I'm going through is a real-life experience.

To grow from this deep and personal death is a mighty blow.

My five senses are in the midst towards the flow.

I just wanted to "Say it right" Nelly Furtado.

Maybe I should "Slow down" Bobby Valentino.

I don't want to go out like my older brother did.

Once I roll up my sleeves while I grieve.

Life itself is so precious.

I do take it very seriously.

By paying my last respects at the funeral.

Funeral arrangements nobody saw this coming.

Everyone that knew Randy paid their last respects.

To think and reflect on the memories they shared together.

During the transaction a sudden rush hits me hard.

Love and support from family and friends.

I have to move on to stay strong.

As the people cheered, they sang praise and worship songs.

I didn't even shed one tear.

Once it hits home, I get a deep chilling sensation.

What does my future hold and reveal?

As I really reflect at the graveyard site.

I can sense your spirit is near me.

I still remember when we fought over the remote control to watch television.

We have a lot of memories inside the living room and kitchen.

The cooking, playing video games, and family gatherings.

You attended North Brandywine Middle School and Coatesville Area Senior High School.

You played basketball at Ash Park.

We ate at the Midway Grille for breakfast.

Those memories and many more will always last.

Randy M. Vaughn's murder did receive justice at the West Chester County Court House in West Chester, Pa.

Closure was given as a guilty verdict was said by Judge Grover E. Koon and the jury.

I'd like to personally thank the Coatesville Police Department, District Attorney, Chester County Detectives Office, Senior Judge Thomas G. Gavin, Tom Hogan, Carlos A. Barraza, and the U.S Marshals.

I thank them for giving my family, members of the community, and the city of Coatesville proper closure.

Nobody deserves to go out on a sad ending due to gun violence.

I wish I had more time with you, my older brother, Randy.

Chapter 13.

Acknowledgements, Appreciation, Recognition, & Thanks

I will be giving Acknowledgements, Thanks, Appreciation, Recognition to the key people, for helping make a tremendous impact in my life. I would like to thank the staff at Brandywine Hospital for helping me stay alive during the labor. I thank the following public-school districts; Coatesville Area School District and the School District of Lancaster for providing me an education as I earned my 5th grade promotion, 8th grade promotion, and graduated from J.P. McCaskey High School.

I want to thank Harrisburg Area Community College for giving me an opportunity to start furthering my education. Millersville University for accepting me as a Transfer Graduate, and the many College Professors, Staff, and Security Officers, and Alumni very much for accepting me as a man making a positive impact.

My path was much different than most college students. I did cross the finish line two times as a college graduate. It was such a high honor being recognized by Dr. Theresa Russell-Loretz with that Special Overcoming Adversity Award.

To my coaches, thanks very much for taking the time to know me outside of being a student athlete. You helped fill in a void in my life with not having a positive male at my home. They say it takes a village to raise a child. Being around my coaches in football, wrestling, and track has allowed me to see men that graduated from college. They provided the blueprint for taking care of their families, and were present in their children's lives. I saw the recipe for success towards being a productive man.

Coach Matt Ortega Sr. is a faithful and caring Husband, Father, and Head Football Coach, & teacher. Thanks very much for being my coach and continuing to stay in contact. I know I made you and your wife very proud when I emailed you my YouTube video of my College Graduation Celebration.

The day we took graduation pictures together speaks high praise and a reflection of the man I have become. It shows our relationship has truly evolved for the better. You have shown me the true meaning of finding the right woman, someone that believes in you, and supports the family all year round. You give thanks to the people behind the scenes such as; your coaching staff, your parents, booster club members, athletic director, student athletes, family, and community leaders.

Dr. Todd Mealy is a proud Husband, Father, Teacher, College Professor, & Author. He taught me so much when I was injured on the freshman football team. After I graduated from high school, and we were staying in contact as our lives entered new chapters. We recently took graduation pictures at his family home. Our relationship has evolved tremendously as we're both Alumni of Millersville University.

Coach Troy Richardson is a man of wisdom, humor, and grit, who taught me to make the most of the opportunity as a student athlete. He always had something new to tell everybody as his loud voice captured the attention of everybody. After high school was over for me, Coach Troy & I remained connected. He is very proud of me for graduating from Harrisburg Area Community College and Millersville University. He truly enjoyed taking graduation pictures with me and embraced me as a man.

Coach Damien Henry was one of my High School Football coaches. My relationship with him has evolved several times over with being a two-time college graduate. For a coach to see the student-athlete that he guided during high school & take College graduation pictures is a proud moment. I showed Coach Damien Henry both college degrees as he smiled. He realized the sacrifices a coach makes for the greater good for the student-athlete's best interest. To see how the fruits of labor have paid off will make him and many other Coaches very proud. He earned his Bachelor's degree from Clarion University.

Coach Kamara was my football and track coach. He's very proud of knowing what I've overcome in my life as he read the front page of the Lancaster Newspaper. As he showed his family members, they felt inspired to know me on a deeper level. Coach Kamara was always present on the J.P. McCaskey High School Campus all year round. He made sure the student-athletes know there's more to life than playing sports. He's a prime example of earning his college degree from Clarion University,

Anh-Hai DuBois was first my neighbor next door to me. Later, we would play video games, two hand touch football, and eat lunch or dinner together. The most memorable moment in my life is when he said I'm like a son to him. I suppose all that time we spent together created that deep of a bond between us. His wife Trina supported his decision to welcome me into his family with open arms and into the home. Thanks very much for being in my life.

Jeremiah Miller is a proud alumnus of Appalachian State College. He works as the J.P. McCaskey High School Alumni Affairs Coordinator Association. I like to thank you very much for allowing me inside the Alumni Office researching the yearbooks for younger pictures of me, and other notable alumni. Thanks very much for attending my 10th year Walking Living Miracle Anniversary.

Kyle Slayermaker (businessman) & Kelly Johnson (professional photographer credit), thanks very much for the Professional

Headshot. You sure do know how to work your magic. Thanks very much for the interview on the Business Brawl as you allowed me to tell my inspirational story.

Mike Sutherland is a proud Alumnus at Hofstra and Iona College at Westchester Community College. Mike is a professional photographer for events, weddings, and special occasions providing services for the clients. Thanks very much for supporting me and inviting me to the networking events. You have allowed me to grow more for meeting new people and providing the Professional Photos for my Walking Living Miracle Anniversaries.

Paul Rodriguez is a father figure and close connection, Thanks very much for believing in me when I practiced for the Lancaster Puerto Rican Parade. We would go over my poem several times at the Puerto Rican Cultural Center. You introduced me to the Board Members of the Puerto Rican Cultural Center and Committee.

Mia Matuszewski is a native of Coatesville, Pa, and a proud alumnus of Coatesville Area Senior High School. Mia and I are childhood friends that grew up in the same neighborhood. Even though I moved to Lancaster, Pa, I still came back to Coatesville to visit her and other people. I remember the days we played sports, games, video games, and fellowshipped together. Her family welcomed me to the cookouts and inside their home. Mia and I made a positive influence in each other's lives, even when we entered new chapters in our lives. I did give her a Mother's Day card and a message inside to show my appreciation.

As we became adults, Mia introduced to the girls she was coaching for her Girls Basketball team, including Demetria Irwin aka Dee – Dee. I made Dee-Dee a poster and attended the basketball games to support her in high school and at Lincoln University.

Shannon Thomas is a proud alumnus of Coatesville Area Senior High School & West Chester University. Shannon is also an independent business owner, an interior decorator and event coordinator. I like to give a big thanks very much for providing your creative vision and services for my Tenth Year Anniversary as a Walking Living Miracle and My book signing day. The guests were really impressed with her designs, colors, and fine linens.

Lizette Matos-Mejia, Mauricio, and family. Thanks very much for attending my College Graduation, and welcoming me into your home, among other things. It all started once me and Lizette matched on Ancestry as cousins. She was the one that initiated for us to meet in person. Meeting your family was an eye-opening experience. As we shared and started taking pictures together the chemistry and bond came naturally. The first impression really did count as it led to more memories created in person.

Michael Pierce, Wife Jackie Pierce, and family Thanks very much for being supportive in my life, allowing me to attend the cookouts, and get a job with the after-school sports programs. You helped me make my transition back into society and make an honest living by having a job. Thanks very much Jackie and family for the time we fellowshipped and created great memories together.

Pauline Tenneh is a proud alumnus of J.P. McCaskey High School and Albright University of Reading, Pa. She competed on the Women's track and field team. Earned a bachelor's degree in Business Administration concentration management. African American Society, Alpha Phi Omega.

Sierra "Ci Ci" Echavarria is a proud alumnus of Penn Manor High School and graduated from Temple University. She was the homecoming queen, singing, and loves poetry. She Earned a bachelor's degree in Psychology concentration Health care Administration and management.

Nesta Anastazia Petit-Ton Martin is a proud alumnus of Garden Spot High School, she was an outstanding track sprinter student athlete, owns many records in the 100, 200-meter dash, she was the team captain. Currently she's a loving mother and faithful wife Nesta Weaver.

Stenid Manning is an alumnus of Reynold Middle School playing field hockey, basketball, and track. She went on to graduate from J.P. McCaskey High School, competing in varsity field hockey, track, and Lancaster City Track Club.

Ariel Jones is a proud alumnus of Cedar Crest High School. She excelled in being a 1,000-point scorer, contributing to the team winning Lancaster-Lebanon Girls Championship. Ariel was very competitive in varsity track as a sprinter and jumper. She went on to further her education at Shippensburg University on an Athletic Scholarship, Ariel succeeded in scoring over 2,000 points, being named P-SAC Women's player of the week and season.

Tyler Crespo is a proud alumnus of Manheim Township High School, he went on to score over 1,000 points, and become the high school all-time leading scorer. He furthered his education at Shippensburg University

---

Janeah Neal is a proud alumnus of Columbia High School, she scored over 1,000 points, was the team captain, and was enrolled in the Attollo Prep program. She went on to further her education at Lock Haven University.

Kahtero Summers graduated from Coatesville Area Senior High School, he played varsity football, track, and basketball. Kahtero went on to graduate from Saint Francis University with a bachelor's degree in business management concentration marketing and related support services, also a Master of business Administration MBA Business.

Julian Collazo is a proud alumnus of Lancaster Mennonite High School, he scored over 1,000 points to become the all-time leader scored, was named Lancaster-Lebanon League Player of the year, and furthered his education at Cairn University. Julian played Collegiate basketball, earned both a bachelor's and master's degree.

Aaron Swinton Jr. is a proud alumnus of J.P. McCaskey High School, he played varsity football and basketball. Graduated from William and Mary university to earn a bachelor's degree in economics and organizational leaderships, also a master's degree in Accounting.

Demetria ``Dee-Dee" Irwin is a proud alumnus of Coatesville Area Senior High School and Lincoln University for nursing. While in high school she scored over 1,000 points and was a team captain.

Edward" Champ" Hall is a proud alumnus of J.P. McCaskey High School. He played varsity football as a running back, sprinter in track, and earned his barber license. Furthering his education at a business school. He's known as the Godfather of Barber School and Haircuts.

Ronald James aka Ron, Thanks very much for being my life coach for providing me the tools to keep me growing as a man. Thanks very much for contributing in my life to level up and make the transition to higher ground.

Dante Shamar McLeod, a native of Philadelphia, Pa, and alumnus of Millersville University. He majored in Sports Journalism. I would like to personally thank you for your contributions towards my Autobiography. Once a marauder, always a marauder.

Eunice Hoefling and family, Thanks very much for allowing me to come over for Thanksgiving and fellowship together. It all started once me and Eunice matched as cousins on ancestry. We connected on social media and decided to meet in person.

Everyone at Lancaster Community Television Station channel 66, Thanks very much for allowing me to complete two internships to gain experience. By interviewing several people, I learned valuable lessons hands-on to create story lines, edit, and give the proper close. Thanks very much for allowing me to be an inspirational story two times on your programming, while I was a college student at Millersville University.

It certainly felt different being interviewed by Jade Grove, alumnus of Lancaster County Day High School & American University. She was a natural, doing the research on me and asking the right questions for the viewers to fully know my story. Jade was very comfortable interviewing me with a flowing conversation that helped me open up more in-depth.

The second interview was more of an updated inspirational story of me as a two-time college graduate and the tenth-year university.

Diane Dayton is a proud alumnus of George Fox University & West Chester University. Also, Frank Altodoerffer, proud alumnus of Manheim Township High School & University of Colorado. Diane has plenty of years of experience as a host, producer, executive producer, and voice over talent, while Frank is more the businessman and enjoyed being behind the scenes. The interview was more professional since it was on Diane Dayton's show called Behind the Lines. I was dressed up in a suit for the special occasion, with a clip and mic.

Ivan C. Bookard 3rd, thanks very much for serving in the Military. It's the brave people like you that make a powerful difference in the world, while people here in America can lay their heads down to rest and live. You have sacrificed countless things to get where you're at now and to be providing for your family. The training camp was a challenge being away from immediate family. You continued to further your education through the United States' Army's WOBC- Warrant Officer Basic Course.

Jason & Nicole McKinney, thanks very much for helping earn my driver's license. With your help I was able to pay it forward to other people in my life. I still remember the day Jason came up to me and said "Ethan I need you to speak your testimony tonight". I was like not feeling comfortable at all since I rarely am called upon to show humility in the public eye, let alone to speak about my lowest point of my life as I hit rock bottom. Looking back now, that situation of being uncomfortable has allowed me to become more comfortable. Maybe I needed that push to grow since I thought everything was over once I got off the feeding tube. In your prayers, you saw visions of more things that I needed to help me become a better man.

The Veronis Family, thanks very much for allowing me into your home for family gatherings & celebrations. I enjoyed the fellowship and giving back to the community, making the world a better place. The Greek fest events make a tremendous impact in several communities around the world. There's plenty of talk time at the table for breakfast, lunch, and dinner as everyone has a voice that truly matters. Everything has an opportunity to speak freely and be cherished in that present moment. Those are fundamental values that help keep a family together all year round.

Ole Hong & Heidi Castillo, thanks very much for helping me create my LLC business at the State Capital of Harrisburg. I believe the timing was right as it was time to get everything legalized. I enjoyed your fellowship at the Lancaster Barnstormers game as I threw out the first pitch.

Barbara Barr, J.P. McCaskey High School, Boston University, & American University. Thanks very much for interviewing me. Highlighting the 10th year Anniversary and everything I've overcome and achieved. We had a wonderful time together at the Attollo office, taking pictures and selfies and showing you my awards. I'm glad you came to my job to record some more b-roll footage.

John Walk, thanks very much for the interview highlighting my 10th year anniversary with an updated story. We had a great time at the Attollo Office to really dive in deep about my personal adversities, sacrifices, and growth of inspiration. That was the most intense interview I've ever had in my life. That Interview was more in depth, beyond the surface with no limitations.

I like to thank the Professional Photographer for coming out to my job at the Coatesville vs J.P. McCaskey Track meet scrimmage. That moment was very special to me and very sincere to my heart. I was born in Coatesville and living in Lancaster half way into my 8th grade year. There was no script written on paper as the photographer was taking my picture. It was special to be photographed there as I was formerly a student-athlete at two Public School Districts, Coatesville Area School District and The School District of Lancaster. I received the best of both worlds to cherish that moment at work and on the high school campus.

I remember people asking me why the photographer was taking several pictures of me. Once I explained everything to the student-athletes and adults were very amazed. They didn't see it coming at all at a track meet scrimmage. I suppose they were surprised with something that was not in the event programming.

Earl "Papa" Boots, Thanks very much for your guidance and support as I transition from Coatesville Area School District to the School District of Lancaster. We had plenty of jokes to tell each other, teachable moments when I needed to respect your words of wisdom, and learn to be present. I enjoyed learning about your journey as a former student athlete at J.P. McCaskey high School. You became a proud father, grandfather, basketball coach, and leader in the community.

Davon Garcia is a Proud Alumni from J.P. McCaskey High School. He played four years of varsity soccer, three years of varsity football, two years of varsity track and field. He further his education and play collegiate soccer at Eastern University. He's a proud father, husband, and gives back to the community to pay it forward. He helped me with my transition with adjusting to living in Lancaster, being a student-athlete, teaching me leadership by example on the J.P. McCaskey High School Campus.

The late great Clyde E. Brown & family, thanks very much for filling in a void in my life when I didn't know I even had one. You held me accountable for my actions just like every other student with no favoritism. We had our moments of laughter, sports talk, history, and shared the experience of being a student-athlete. Even though you have passed away. I'm still connected with your family members to this present day. In your final days I made the time to visit you inside the Lancaster General Hospital & Manor Care nursing home.

The late Curtis Jefferson and family, who watched me get baptized as I gave my life to Christ for a new start. He allowed me to be myself as I listened to him speak life into me. The timing was everything as we grew closer and he introduced me to his family. I ended up following your Granddaughter's student athlete journey, as she went on to have great team success and earn an Athletic Scholarship to further her education and play Women's Collegiate Basketball.

I remember the day I saw Jordan S. Steffy inside church on a Saturday night. He sat right next to me, and I was very surprised indeed. After we exchanged contact information and connected on social media, our lives benefited each other for many more years to come. He planted positive seeds in me as a grown man by taking me on a college tour visiting several campuses on the east coast. Jordan allowed me to contribute towards fundraising events, visit his family, be introduced to his mentors, and meet very important people believing in his vision.

I earned his trust when he sent me on trips with his credit card, cash, car keys, and allowed me into his home. Kiandra is his loving Wife, Life Partner, and nourishing Mother to their children. Kiandra & I attended J.P. McCaskey High School together. Jordan & Kiandra, thanks very much for paying it forward as your mentors paid it forward to you.

I want to thank my African, European, Indian, and Puerto Rican ancestors for paving the way for the generations that came after them. I am one of several men that actually graduated from college with two degrees. I understand times have changed over the years with the Federal laws for protection against discrimination, racism, and other things.

There was a high cost to pay for more blessings and better opportunities for the future generations. Some didn't experience things some people take for granted today and others continue to fight for such as owning a home, land, starting a business, earning a high school diploma, college degrees, playing sports, or being protected from racism, and discrimination.

They knew life had to be much better to pass the torch on down. My ancestors have left a blueprint for overcoming adversities by turning them to their advantage. Their legacies will always be remembered and acknowledged. As they've touched and impacted millions of lives for over hundreds of years.

Afterword

Thank you very much for taking the time to read my inspirational book. I hope the investment of your time and money was worth it. In return, I hope that, by reading my book, you have gained knowledge, wisdom, and common sense to change your life. If I meet you in person in the near future. Have your book ready for me to sign with a black sharpie, show me the notes you took, underlying text, and we could take a picture together.

In your free time, please check my website ethanspeaks.com, because I can upload examples, templates, resources for you to review, and maybe use in your life. I believe my book has truly inspired you to overcome your own personal situations. I remember an old saying "You cannot be what you cannot see". Now that you have taken the time to read my inspirational story come to light.

You, the reader, can feel encouraged to do more in your life and others. Now that you've learned of my personal challenges, you have the blueprint to overcome any hindrance in your own life. I hope you are truly touched beyond curiosity and expanded your mind to new possibilities ahead to persevere and become successful in your own life.

My story hopefully opens up the lines of communication and inquiry the importance of mental health, justice for the people, more resources for the youth, and provide proper representation in having honest conversations to experience breakthroughs. While I have made plenty of efforts in my life, there's still more things that need to be achieved, and the right tools to pass on down to future generations. Feel free to follow me on all social media platforms to stay connected with me.

The true comeback story in the 21st century is your lifetime. You can find your greatness with the purpose for your own life.

Invest into my book, you'll truly feel the inspirational verb and vibe.

I have lived long to see the outpouring of people. To see the impact of my autobiography, documentary, movie, and soundtrack. Hopefully my story has bridged the gap to inspire people around the globe. My dreams are kept open to travel across the world. Take up the mantle to forgo your own path, find what is worthwhile for yourself. My proud achievements are a true reflecting of everything I've earned.

Author's Biography

Ethan A. Poetic, native of Coatesville, Pennsylvania graduated from JP McCaskey High School in Lancaster, Pennsylvania. Ethan has also graduated from Harrisburg Area Community College with an Associate's degree in General Studies. He graduated from Millersville University with a Bachelor's of Science Degree with a major Speech Communications and a minor in Broadcasting and Media.

Ethan received two Pennsylvania Commonwealth citations, Proclamation Declaration from Mayor Danene Sorace, and Lancaster City Council members.
Ethan was featured in the Lancaster Newspaper (LNP) Writer John Walk and featured on WGAL for his inspirational story Reporter Barbara Barr.

Ethan currently works for the Substitute Teacher Service as a teacher's assistant and personal care paraprofessional. He is active in community events and is a positive influence to the youth and started his own business Ethan A. Poetic,LLC to use his story to empower people to overcome their own adversities.

Ethan's story is about overcoming a near fatal car accident, facing 99% of death vs. 1% of life. Ethan, with the power of prayer, hard work, determination, and courage reclaimed his life. Ethan desires to be a Keynote Speaker, producer, daytime television presenter, sports anchor, and conduct interviews with student athletes, and leaders.

Ethan has inspired many young people, leaders, family members, law enforcement agencies, and college campuses across the United States of America.

Coatesville Facts and Notable people

Coatesville, Pa was voted to become a city in 1915, and in the mid 1700's the Fleming Family were early owners of land. The property was purchased by Moses Coates in 1787. He was a farmer, inventor, and first postmaster. The city is named after Moses Coates. The Lukens Steel Company forged the steel beams for the World Trade Center in New York City; Presently owned by Cleveland-Cliffs Inc.

The Coatesville Historic District, Veterans Affairs Medical Center, Lukens Historic District are one of many sites listed as a National Register of Historic places.

In 1929 The VA Medical Center was built to provide neuropsychiatric care to veterans from the military. Coatesville is served by the Coatesville Amtrak Station, and SEPTA (Southeastern Pennsylvania Transportation Authority), Notable people of Coatesville, Pa are Richard Hamilton, Billy Joe, Walt Downing Jr., Vince Belnome, John Adrian Gibney Jr. Hubie Marshall, Calvin Grove, Ray Keech, Rodney Linderman, Rebecca Lukens, first American Female CEO in the industrial company. Charles Hewes Moore Jr., Roderick Maurice Perry, Susan Richardson, Fred Masherino,

www.ingramcontent.com/pod-product-compliance
Lightning Source LLC
Chambersburg PA
CBHW020439130626
46549CB00001B/214
9798986847207